"If you long to free yourself from the trance of addiction, this brilliantly organized workbook will guide you with compassion and clarity. *Sober Starting Today Workbook* combines transformational mindfulness practices with the wisdom of Western psychology to offer readers a practical, hopeful path toward deep healing and self-awareness."

> —**Tara Brach, PhD**, author of *Radical Acceptance* and *Trusting the Gold*

"Whether you're trying to quit, cut back, or just take a break from using substances, you'll need self-compassion for your journey, and no workbook lays out that path with simple, straightforward practices better than Deborah Sosin's *Sober Starting Today Workbook*."

> —**Christopher Willard, PsyD**, part-time faculty at Harvard Medical School, and author of *How We Grow Through What We Go Through*

"In this beautifully written and organized workbook, Deborah Sosin addresses the subject of addiction in a way that artfully links the practice of mindfulness with the journey of recovery as powerful cofactors in healing. Readers and practitioners who complete the book's exercises and practice embodied awareness as they are guided will have a new experience of their habits. Guaranteed."

> —**Lawrence Peltz, MD**, author of *The Mindful Path to Addiction Recovery*

"This clinical workbook is a must-read not only for people suffering from addiction, but for the people who love them. It offers a richly user-friendly approach to providing the skills people need for achieving substance reduction and abstinence. With its helpful vignettes and essential worksheets, this book addresses the core question asked by those struggling with alcohol and drugs: 'How do I get control of my addiction?'"

> —**Michael W. Otto, PhD**, professor of psychology at Boston University, and author of *Exercise for Mood and Anxiety Disorders*

"Deborah Sosin's *Sober Starting Today Workbook* is packed cover to cover with practical wisdom and exercises to help people achieve and maintain recovery. Her mindfulness-based guidance is readily combined with other interventions, for example, 12-step groups. While based on Buddhist tradition, two foundation stones to what Deborah offers—namely, compassion and hope—are crucial components to other belief systems also, so her language is familiar and comforting. I recommend this workbook to colleagues and patients."

> —**Mark J. Albanese, MD**, medical director at Massachusetts Physician Health Services, and faculty in the department of psychiatry at Harvard Medical School/Cambridge Health Alliance

"Deborah Sosin does a great job offering evidence-based mindfulness and cognitive behavioral therapy (CBT) strategies to assist clients on their recovery journeys. The 'Does This Sound Like You?' component is an excellent way for clients to compare their personal situations to real-life scenarios. Although designed for clients, the book also offers activities that will help counselors in their clinical work."

> —**Patrick Griswold, MEd, MSN, RN, LAC**, associate professor in the department of human services and counseling, and clinical instructor in the department of nursing at Metropolitan State University of Denver

"*Sober Starting Today Workbook* is a refreshing, forgiving, yet realistic and hopeful step-by-step guide for navigating the addiction recovery journey. This workbook is well paced and logically sequenced with real-life examples applicable to anyone. It is respectful of the disorder and the person. It introduces valuable life-coping skills that are useful to anyone looking for a comprehensive self-care guide and resource."

      —**Janice Kauffman, RN, MPH, LADC**, assistant professor of psychiatry at Harvard Medical School

"Deborah Sosin's *Sober Starting Today Workbook* does what most recovery-focused books do not—it integrates a wide range of evidence-based tools into a clear, easy-to-access sequence so that someone can be well supported in either entering or deepening their recovery experience."

      —**Mitch Abblett, PhD**, psychologist; and author of the Nautilus Gold Award-Winning mindful parenting book, *Prizeworthy*

# SOBER STARTING TODAY

## WORKBOOK

### Powerful Mindfulness & CBT Tools to Help You Break Free from Addiction

Deborah Sosin, MSW, LICSW

New Harbinger Publications, Inc.

## Publisher's Note

NEW HARBINGER PUBLICATIONS is a registered trademark of New Harbinger Publications, Inc.

New Harbinger Publications is an employee-owned company.

Copyright © 2024 by Deborah Sosin
New Harbinger Publications, Inc.
5720 Shattuck Avenue
Oakland, CA 94609
www.newharbinger.com

All Rights Reserved

Cover design by Amy Shoup

Acquired by Jess O'Brien

Edited by Jean Blomquist

Library of Congress Cataloging-in-Publication Data on file

Printed in the United States of America

26    25    24

10    9    8    7    6    5    4    3    2    1          First Printing

# Contents

## THE MIND-BODY CONNECTION

## LOOK BACK AND LOOK AHEAD

# Foreword

When Deborah Sosin asked if I would be willing to write a foreword for this workbook, I said, "How can I say no?" I've known Debbie for many years—she was a participant in the first Mindful Self-Compassion course I co-led in 2010, and she has remained a valued colleague in both the MSC community and the Institute for Meditation and Psychotherapy. It's an honor to contribute a few words to this thoughtful book.

Working with clients who are in recovery from addiction is a challenging venture, requiring a solid grasp of the complex and ever-evolving web of medical, psychological, and sociological factors as well as the growing range of treatment options for people seeking help. Most important is approaching the work with an abundance of patience and empathy—because, bottom line, change is hard for everyone. And *how* we engage in the change process has a big impact on the outcome.

The beauty of this book is that the reader is exposed to simple yet profound ideas and practices that really work. Debbie's approach is personal, warm, and grounded in solid science. She offers a creative and beautifully organized array of exercises—beginning, wisely, with "Mindfulness as Your Anchor." Mindfulness, or moment-to-moment awareness, is an inner capacity that can make every aspect of our lives easier.

But mindfulness is not just awareness—it's kind and compassionate awareness. People often use substances to avoid how they're feeling, especially when they feel bad about themselves. Substances can temporarily alleviate feelings such as anxiety, anger, grief, shame, or guilt, but they can also engender even more painful feelings and lead to devastating consequences. The way out of this conundrum is compassion, especially self-compassion.

This book is deeply compassionate in both style and content. In addition to learning about your triggers, identifying reasons not to use, and transforming negative thoughts and feelings, you will learn to care for yourself in new, healthy ways in such exercises as "Creating a Safe Network," "Your Nutrition and Sleep," and "Reexamining Your Relationships." Two specific exercises invite you to gently begin a self-compassion practice.

You will also learn to develop a more supportive, empowered inner voice, as shown in "Dear Self…Yes, You!", "Revising Your Inner Dialogue," and—one of my favorites—a daily exercise called "The Big Brag." If you've been struggling with low self-worth for many years, practicing self-compassion, much less bragging about your strengths and positive qualities, may seem strange or uncomfortable. However, through practice, I believe that we're all capable of becoming better, kinder friends to ourselves. In fact, recent research strongly supports the benefits of self-compassion. The cognitive behavioral therapy (CBT) techniques offered in this book have been carefully selected from a wide range of these scientifically proven strategies. We can think of mindfulness and self-compassion as the latest additions to the CBT toolbox, also known as "third-wave" treatments.

Another unique feature of this book is the premise that through cultivating the resources of mindfulness and compassion, *any* approach to overcoming addiction can be strengthened. That is, readers who are inclined toward the philosophies of 12-step programs will discover concepts and practices that can be easily integrated into their sobriety efforts. And for those who are more inclined toward traditional psychotherapy or who are trying to become sober on their own, this book will also be a valuable companion.

As you will see, Debbie is a talented clinician and writer (two skills that don't necessarily go together). Her voice is clear, encouraging, and never preachy, honoring the free will and wisdom of the reader at every turn. Whether you are just starting out on your path to sobriety, or well along but seeking additional tools, or exploring the landscape of recovery without quite being ready to commit to change, I believe you will find the practices in this book highly accessible, refreshingly simple, and perhaps even life changing. So why wait?

—Christopher Germer, PhD
Lecturer on Psychiatry, Harvard Medical School
Co-developer of the *Mindful Self-Compassion* program

# Introduction

If you are among the millions of Americans struggling with drugs or alcohol, seeking help is one of the bravest things you'll ever do. It is an expression of empowerment, a way to claim more control over your life, especially in these uncertain, challenging times. But what is the best path to sobriety? While some experts might insist they know "the answer," there *is* no right answer. In other words, one size does not fit all. Some people who follow a rigid model end up relapsing. Some who try on their own do just fine.

In the past twenty years, I have worked with hundreds of clients in outpatient individual and group therapy and at a community methadone clinic. I have heard their stories and their pain, their hopes and dreams. I have seen some of them succeed in sobriety and some fail. A number have died as a result of their addiction, despite their fervent efforts to change.

This workbook is intended for people who are concerned about the negative consequences of their substance use and are looking for practical, effective exercises to guide them toward sobriety. The term *sobriety* here, in its simplest definition, refers to physical abstinence from mind-altering substances that lead to negative consequences; but living a sober life involves much more than abstinence, as you will see. Please note that in this book, sobriety does *not* refer to the cessation of medications to treat chemical dependency that are prescribed by a doctor, nor does it refer to stopping medications properly prescribed to treat co-occurring psychiatric conditions. This book draws on multiple philosophies and approaches, with an emphasis on mindfulness and cognitive behavioral therapy (CBT). You'll learn relapse prevention strategies. You'll practice how to be more compassionate with yourself, how to better manage your thoughts and feelings, how to set limits and deal with difficult situations and people, and how to chart a course for a happier, healthier life—the life you really want.

## WHAT IS ADDICTION?

When we think of substance addiction, we often think of the chemical-based factors that compel someone to use, marked by increased tolerance (needing more to get the same effect) and/or withdrawal symptoms, such as nausea, vomiting, shakes, and so on, that people might experience upon cutting back or quitting. In those cases, inpatient detox is considered the treatment of choice.

But not everyone with problem substance use shows such signs of physical addiction. People who are not chemically dependent can also struggle with cravings, mental obsessions, or other compulsive behaviors that can lead to relapse. Research shows that the brain can, over time, hijack one's sense of control, perhaps because of damage to certain brain receptors. To understand addiction better, neuroscientists are also investigating the highly complex interactions among the brain's reward and control systems as well as studying how behaviors are influenced not only by chemicals but by habit, repetition, reinforcement, and so on (National Institute on Drug Abuse 2022).

In this book, *addiction* is defined as ongoing, often compulsive use of a harmful substance despite negative consequences, with or without chemical dependence. Also, this book uses the term *substance use* as opposed to *substance abuse*, which has a negative, punitive connotation. By introducing less pejorative terminology, I hope to break through the historical stigma associated with drug and alcohol addiction and bring more compassion and understanding to both the discussion and the treatment of this devastating problem in our culture.

# HOW TO USE THIS WORKBOOK

This workbook offers therapeutic exercises to help you learn about your substance use, make healthy choices, practice new skills, and try strategies to prevent relapse. There is a logical sequence to the exercises in this book, but you may also jump around and do the ones you find the most relevant and useful.

There are nine sections of exercises. Each section will help you learn a specific set of skills. For each exercise, there is a purpose and a brief overview of the topic called "Did You Know?" Then you'll find a short vignette called "Does This Sound Like You?" This is followed by an exercise or activity titled "What to Do."

> **Note:** The fictional vignettes are intended to illustrate a range of real-life stories about people of different ages, classes, genders, races, ethnicities, sexual preference, choice of substances, and severity of use. As is often the case with such vignettes, events and outcomes are condensed for purposes of brevity. In real life, recovery from addiction is naturally less linear and more complex.

You might consider keeping a journal as you work through this book, to jot down reflections, insights, memories, goals, or any other thoughts. You might also identify areas in which you'd like to progress.

Let's take a brief look at each of the nine sections:

- **Start on the Path to Sobriety.** You'll begin your journey with two exercises. First, you'll learn about mindfulness—what it means and how it can be a useful anchor for not only your recovery but also your entire life. Then, you'll write a vision statement, which gives you the opportunity to look forward and create a picture of what you want your life to be.

- **Get Ready.** As you begin exploring what to do about your problem substance use, the exercises in this section will help you to identify your personal pros and cons for both using and not using. You'll learn about the Stages of Change model and begin a conversation with the different parts of yourself through a guided letter-writing exercise.

- **Know Your Triggers.** Here, you'll begin to identify your internal and external triggers and how to manage urges and cravings. Then you'll have a chance to get clear about your reasons for starting on the path to sobriety.

- **Take Action.** The exercises in this section will help you identify specific things you can do in the early stages of recovery, including limiting your access to substances as well as identifying and practicing alternatives to using. You'll also learn the PLAN strategy for attending potential triggering events such as family reunions, holidays, work meetings, weddings, and parties.

- **Build a Safety Net.** Most experts agree that working a recovery program is nearly impossible to do alone. Creating a safe network of supportive people can help you set the stage for long-term success. In this section, you'll work on identifying specific people, places, actions, and activities to enhance your recovery efforts. You'll also learn strategies for asking for help and setting up accountability, and how to stretch outside your comfort zone despite fears and doubts.

- **Know Your Feelings.** What is the range of human emotions and feelings, and how can you learn to experience, and even accept, all those feelings without picking up? In this section, you'll work on identifying pleasant and unpleasant feelings, and then practice noticing and recording the different feelings you might experience on a given day, such as fear, anger, anxiety, boredom, sadness, shame, guilt, and loss, as well as happiness and serenity. You'll also learn the difference between "reacting" and "responding" to events and experiences, and you'll write a letter to your substance of choice.

- **Know Your Thoughts.** In this section, you'll learn about the powerful relationship between your thoughts and feelings and how to use that awareness to prevent a relapse. Drawing from the world of cognitive behavioral therapy, one exercise will help you notice and label your thoughts. You'll learn about the power of self-compassion as a key to good recovery—and a good life. Then you'll practice techniques for creating a new inner dialogue—noticing old, habitual negative messages and building a repertoire of new go-to thoughts that will drive you toward positive, healthy choices.

- **The Mind-Body Connection.** The exercises in this section offer you the opportunity to explore new, healthy ways of treating your body, mind, and spirit, including breathing exercises, relaxation exercises, mindful movement, and mindful eating. You'll explore some strategies for eating well and sleeping better. Next, you'll have the opportunity to learn additional self-compassion practices for the treatment of shame. Finally, you'll learn about the formal practice of mindful meditation as well as informal mindfulness practices.

- **Look Back and Look Ahead.** There's a lot to be said for taking one day at a time, but sometimes it's useful to look back and review where you've come from and how your past can inform your future. In this section, you'll review your current and past relationships and assess how they might be supportive or unsupportive in your recovery efforts. You'll write a second letter to yourself, identify your strengths and passions, learn about how to maintain HOPE, and write a second vision statement to support a lifetime of recovery.

Following the nine main sections, you will also find reproducible Daily Exercises, a list of Additional Resources, and Words of Wisdom:

- **Daily Exercises.** The four exercises in this section are different from the others in this workbook, as they are intended to be used every day, or as often as possible. Setting goals, acknowledging challenges, practicing gratitude, and celebrating accomplishments can be key to your recovery, keeping you on track and engaged actively on the path to sobriety with clear, actionable steps. You can photocopy these exercises or, if you prefer, you can download them at http://www.newharbinger.com/52762. You will also find many of the exercises and worksheets from the main sections of the book on this website, including two audio recordings of guided meditations with relaxing music. For more details, see the very back of this book.

- **Additional Resources.** This section provides an overview of some additional options you may choose in your recovery process. Under "Getting Professional Help," you will learn about inpatient and outpatient programs, medications for addiction treatment, and other interventions. Under "Finding Self-Help Programs," you will learn about the many free, community-based programs and groups that are available in person and online.

- **Words of Wisdom.** This final section includes a gallery of inspiring and helpful phrases drawn primarily from the Alcoholics Anonymous program, with room to create your own, too.

## A FINAL WORD BEFORE YOU BEGIN

The tools in this book are designed to help people achieve abstinence from any self-administered, mind-altering substances that lead to negative consequences in one's life. Although some people might benefit from cutting back or moderating their use of drugs or alcohol without quitting entirely, I have noticed that those who choose sobriety, with or without the help of AA or other programs, feel better, do better, and have the energy and clearheadedness to move forward in all areas of their lives—physical, emotional, social, professional, and spiritual.

Whether you do the exercises on your own or with a skilled therapist, or as part of an addiction treatment program, I hope this book can be a companion on your journey toward sobriety, starting today.

# Start on the Path to Sobriety

# I  Mindfulness as Your Anchor

*PURPOSE:* To gain a basic understanding of mindfulness by practicing a simple breathing exercise and a grounding exercise.

## DID YOU KNOW?

Mindfulness is everywhere, from mainstream magazines to digital media to elementary school classrooms to employee assistance programs. More and more people are seeking ways to calm their minds and bodies, reduce stress, and be more effective in their daily lives. It might sound like a New Age-y trend, but mindfulness is actually more than 2,500 years old, stemming from ancient Buddhist traditions.

The term *mindfulness* refers to the practice of *noticing what's happening right here and now, without judgment and with acceptance*—to which you might say, "Easier said than done!" But you can learn.

Addiction or no addiction, many of us go through our days in a trancelike state, on automatic pilot, unaware of what's really happening in the present moment. We spend too much time thinking about the past or worrying about the future. Or we distract ourselves by compulsively checking our phones, watching TV, or, for our purposes here, using mind-altering substances. When we're in that trance, we're checked out, or *mindless.*

"I don't want to pay attention to what's going on right here and now—it's too stressful," some people say. Or too painful. Or scary. Or sad. That can be true at first, especially if you're used to tuning out the present moment through using substances. But there's hope!

This workbook offers specific strategies for using mindfulness to help you cope better in the here and now. Throughout your journey toward sobriety, you are invited to turn to mindfulness as your anchor. You may find that your relationship to your problem drug or alcohol use may change as you get better at noticing, being present, not judging, and accepting.

Mindfulness has other benefits, too:

- Improves mood
- Boosts self-esteem
- Increases resilience
- Reduces depression and anxiety
- Boosts concentration, attention, and memory
- Improves learning and creativity
- Boosts immune system and cardiovascular health
- Helps with chronic pain
- Helps with sleep and eating habits
- Reduces stress
- Heightens sense of being alive

And did you know that mindfulness can literally change the brain? Studies have shown that a regular mindfulness practice can lead to an increase in the gray matter in the prefrontal cortex, which has to do with problem solving, decision making, hypothesizing, and strategizing, as well as in the hippocampus, which regulates emotions and behaviors (Singleton et al. 2014). And, even better, mindfulness can shrink the activity in the amygdala, the "fight-flight-freeze" part of the brain that is aroused when detecting and reacting to emotions, especially fear.

We would need a separate book to delve further into not only the neurology of mindfulness but also the complex neurology of addiction. But this basic information can be useful as you learn more about how mindfulness can help you recover from problem drug and alcohol use.

## DOES THIS SOUND LIKE YOU?

*Jonathan, 39, a database manager, has always enjoyed alcohol and never thought of himself as a problem drinker. In the past, he only permitted himself to drink on weekends, but ever since he and his wife adopted a child, his anxiety has spiked. He started having one or two, sometimes three, cocktails in the evening after work. Now he's more irritable and frequently falls asleep before the baby's bedtime. In the morning, he notices his heart is beating faster and he often has a headache. Jonathan's wife is concerned about his bad moods and escalating drinking, especially because Jonathan's father also has a history of problem drinking. She is urging him to cut back on his alcohol use and take a stress management class.*

How are you like Jonathan? How are you different?

_____

_____

_____

What do you think Jonathan should do in this situation? What can you imagine yourself doing?

_____

_____

_____

## WHAT TO DO

Below are two mindfulness exercises—one involves noticing the body and the breath; the other involves using your senses to notice things outside the body. Many stress management and mindfulness teachers recommend noticing the breath to anchor yourself in the present moment. "Take Three Conscious Breaths" is a great starting point.

For many people, focusing on the breath can trigger some discomfort or anxiety. If that's the case for you, that's fine. Don't judge yourself for "failing" at breathing. Instead, try the other exercise below, "5-4-3-2-1 Grounding," which is a different way of being present in the moment.

Of course, you can practice both exercises and switch them up as needed as you build skills for sobriety. Later, in the section titled "The Mind-Body Connection," you'll find additional mindfulness exercises to expand your repertoire.

## Take Three Conscious Breaths

Sit comfortably in a chair and take an easy breath. Read this paragraph through, then close your eyes. Notice what you're feeling in your body and mind. Let go of any tension you're aware of. And breathe—three slow, easy, deep, conscious breaths, expanding your lungs fully, holding for a second or two, then exhaling slowly. Notice any physical sensations, any thoughts or judgments, and see if you can let them go, too.

What was that like for you? Write down your responses here.

_____

_____

_____

Mindfulness isn't only about breathing, as we'll discuss later in this book, but it's a good way to practice noticing what's happening right here and now. Pick a regular time every day when you can commit to taking three conscious breaths. For example, you could do it each time you wake up, open your front door, go to the bathroom, park your car, or arrive home. Notice what's happening in that moment. Then record the experience in the chart below.

| Take Three Conscious Breaths/When? | Where? | What did you notice? | How did it feel? |
|---|---|---|---|
| Example: Before I get dressed | Sitting on the bed | Breathing slowed down, belly relaxed, eyes softened | Relaxing! Less anxiety. |
| | | | |
| | | | |
| | | | |
| | | | |

If you'd like to continue working with this exercise, you may download a worksheet at http://www.newharbinger .com/52762.

## 5-4-3-2-1 Grounding

Another easy mindfulness practice involves engaging all five senses to notice what is in your immediate environment—starting with using one sense to notice five items, then switching senses as you count down to just noticing one item. Focusing outward is a great way to ground your mind and body in the present—and to remember that the world around you offers many sources of calm, pleasure, and peace.

You can practice this exercise anytime, anywhere. "5-4-3-2-1 Grounding" can serve as another anchor throughout your day—that is, you don't have to wait until you "need" to ground yourself as a reaction to some upsetting or stressful event. You can train your mind and body to be more aware in a pleasant, neutral way even when nothing stressful is happening. Record your experiences in the chart that follows.

### 5: SIGHT

Notice *five* things that you can see with your eyes right now. It might be your floor, your clothing, a painting on your wall, the birds or trees outside your window, and so on.

### 4: TOUCH

Select *four* things that you would like to touch: a blanket, a dish, a pillow, a flower, a lamp. Close your eyes and really take in the different textures and qualities of each object. Is it hard? Soft? Rough? Smooth? Notice the temperature. How does it feel on your skin?

### 3: SOUND

Tune in to the sounds around you. What are *three* things that you hear? A ticking clock? The refrigerator's hum? Chirping birds? A passing car? The sounds might be pleasant or unpleasant—it doesn't matter. Using your sense of hearing can help you concentrate on something outside yourself and help you feel more grounded in the present.

### 2: SMELL

What *two* smells can you identify in your environment? If it's hard to smell something specific while you're sitting still, you might walk around and choose—maybe it's a flower or a soap scent or a pet smell or fresh fruit. Inhale deeply through your nose and experience with total focus the smell of those two objects.

### 1: TASTE

Taste *one* thing and taste it fully and slowly. It could be a sip of tea or coffee, a bite of cheese, a raspberry, a square of chocolate. Whatever you choose to taste mindfully for this exercise, pay full attention to that moment and that item. Relax. Enjoy.

Try practicing this exercise daily for the next week and record your experiences below. You may return to this exercise as your anchor at any point in your process.

| Day | 5-4-3-2-1 Grounding: When and where? | 5 things you saw? 4 things you touched? 3 things you heard? 2 things you smelled? 1 thing you tasted? | What did you notice? How did it feel? |
|---|---|---|---|
| Sunday | | | |
| Monday | | | |
| Tuesday | | | |
| Wednesday | | | |
| Thursday | | | |
| Friday | | | |
| Saturday | | | |

If you'd like to continue working with this exercise, you'll find a downloadable worksheet at http://www.new harbinger.com/52762.

# 2 Vision Statement, Part I

*PURPOSE:* To generate a sense of hope by creating a vision of what you'd like your life to look like in six months, one year, and two years.

## DID YOU KNOW?

Whenever we make a big change in our lives, it's easy to feel overwhelmed. In making the decision to stop using drugs or alcohol, you might feel excited, but you might also feel anxious or sad. That's normal and understandable. With all those difficult feelings, it's hard to get in touch with a sense of hope—hope for success, hope for relief from the addiction, and hope for a happier future. It's okay to hope, even if you're going through a tough time—maybe *especially* then. A vision of your future can serve as a powerful guidepost along your road to sobriety. That's why this exercise appears at the beginning of your process.

## DOES THIS SOUND LIKE YOU?

*Ariella, 24, had been drinking to excess since her senior year in high school. Although she graduated from college with a degree in computer science, her drinking escalated rapidly after graduation, and she didn't pursue a job in her chosen field. She attended different outpatient programs and has now been sober for two months, attends AA, and has a sponsor. She is working as a barista in a café. Ariella wants to stay sober and is trying to live "one day at a time," but when she thinks about her future, it looks like a big, blank slate.*

How are you like Ariella? How are you different?

_____

_____

_____

Do you know what you want in your life? Is there anything in the way of your working toward what you want? Describe briefly.

_____

_____

_____

# WHAT TO DO

In this exercise, you'll create a vision statement to help you "keep your eyes on the prize"— living a happier life.

First, make a list of twelve things you want in your life. There are no right or wrong answers, and you don't have to be realistic. Just go for it, whether it's getting a job, moving to a new place, buying a house, taking a vacation, falling in love, having children, or simply having peace of mind—anything goes! Use extra paper if needed. If you want, you can create a collage of images from magazines or download photos or images from the internet instead. Again, it's okay to dream and hope. You deserve it!

**Things I Want in My Life:**

1. _____

2. _____

3. _____

4. _____

5. _____

6. _____

7. _____

8. _____

9. _____

10. _____

11. _____

12. _____

How did that feel? Was it fun or stressful or a little bit of both? Write your response here:

_____

_____

_____

_____

_____

Now you'll create your vision statement. You'll have the chance to do this exercise twice in this workbook. This time, you'll focus on your vision for six months, one year, and two years from today. Later, you'll think even further into the future. You may refer to your list of wants to help you shape your statement.

These are some categories you might want to include:

- Relationship to drugs and/or alcohol (using/not using)

- Relationships with friends

- Relationships with family

- Intimate relationships

- Health

- Finances

- Job/school

- Spirituality

The key is to write in the present tense, *pretending* it is actually six months, one year, or two years from now. Here is Ariella's six-month vision statement:

*"I haven't had a drink in eight months. I feel better and happier. I have a wonderful support group at AA—I can tell them anything. I'm still working at the café and saving some money. I'm taking an advanced computer-programming class and thinking about where I might want to apply for a good job in the computer science field. Things are looking hopeful!"*

## My Six-Month Vision Statement

_____

_____

_____

_____

_____

_____

_____

_____

_____

## My One-Year Vision Statement

_____

_____

_____

_____

_____

_____

_____

_____

## My Two-Year Vision Statement

_____

_____

_____

_____

_____

_____

_____

_____

# Get Ready

# 3 Weighing Your Pros and Cons—with a Twist

*PURPOSE:* To move toward making a decision about your problem substance use by creating a chart identifying your pros and cons for both using and not using.

## DID YOU KNOW?

Do you have mixed feelings about whether to quit using drugs or alcohol? Probably. And that's completely normal. In fact, recognizing and articulating your mixed feelings can help you decide what to do next. This means being willing to take a good, honest look at *all* aspects of your behavior, your pros and your cons.

Some might worry that acknowledging the pros of substance use is wrong or risky. For instance, if you were to say to a loved one who has expressed concern, "Alcohol takes the edge off my anxiety," or "Heroin makes me feel euphoric," or "Cocaine fuels my creativity," you're likely to get into a nasty argument, which won't help you in your decision-making process.

This exercise is not about right or wrong or good or bad. It's called a *decisional balance exercise*, developed by psychologists James Prochaska and colleagues (Prochaska et al. 1994). It is designed to help you understand and accept your *true, ambivalent feelings without any value judgment*. Completing this exercise can be powerfully effective for people in recovery.

The twist of this exercise is that you'll be naming your pros and cons for both using *and* not using. You'll identify what you get out of using and what you're afraid of losing if you decide to quit. Exploring your mixed feelings from this unusual angle frequently leads to fresh insights.

Are you ready? Let's get started! The more familiar you are with your own complex feelings and perceptions, the more freedom you'll have to make smart, healthy decisions going forward.

## DOES THIS SOUND LIKE YOU?

*Melanie, 19, is a freshman in college. Alcohol is in abundant supply on her campus. Most weekends, Melanie can be found partying with her friends until the wee hours of the morning. Even though Melanie drinks about as much as her friends do, she gets a lot drunker a lot faster and has been known to pass out and not remember what happened. She even woke up in the hospital emergency room once because her friends couldn't rouse her, so they called 911. Her parents have threatened to pull her out of school and send her to a treatment program. Melanie is a little concerned about this pattern, but she doesn't want to feel like a total social outcast if she doesn't drink or go to parties.*

How are you like Melanie? How are you different?

_____

_____

_____

What do you think Melanie should do about her drinking?

_____

_____

_____

# WHAT TO DO

This exercise is an opportunity to zero in on what you see as the pros (benefits) and cons (costs) of your substance use from different angles. You might consider the following categories in choosing your responses: physical, emotional, financial, relational, spiritual, sexual, legal, social, professional, and academic, among others.

Here is a sample box that Melanie filled out, to give you an idea of how it works. The asterisks will be explained later.

| Status | Pros (Benefits) | Cons (Costs) |
|---|---|---|
| **Using** | • Easier to socialize<br>• Feel relaxed*<br>• It's fun<br>• Helps me sleep<br>• Don't have to deal with problems<br>• Less nervous/anxious<br>• Fit in with the crowd | • Hospitalized for alcohol poisoning<br>• Spending too much<br>• Parents are upset<br>• One fender bender<br>• Weight gain<br>• Blacking out<br>• Might have to go to a treatment program* |
| **Not Using** | • Clearheaded<br>• No hangovers<br>• Parents would be happier*<br>• Schoolwork would be easier<br>• Feel better about myself | • Social anxiety*<br>• Facing my problems<br>• Feeling irritable all the time<br>• Not sleeping well<br>• Having to be responsible |

Now it's your turn. Pick one box. It doesn't matter which one. Ignore all the other boxes for the moment. Write down all the things you can think of for that category. Drop any shame, guilt, self-criticism, or worry about how your ideas might sound—just be as honest and uninhibited as you can. Let it out! When you start to run out of ideas, move to another box and focus on that one. You might notice some overlap, but that's okay. Just keep writing until you feel you're done. Quantity doesn't matter. You might have two items in one box and twenty in another. That's all right. When you have filled in each box to the best of your ability, reread your list, one box at a time. Add any new items that come to mind.

| Status | Pros (Benefits) | Cons (Costs) |
|---|---|---|
| Using | | |
| Not Using | | |

Now, in each box, put an asterisk next to the item that feels the *most important* to you from an emotional standpoint—that is, the one that has the strongest "kick." Be honest. For example, in her pros of using box, Melanie asterisked "Feel relaxed"; in her cons of using box, she asterisked "Might have to go to a treatment program." These answers gave her important information that could help motivate her to change.

Compare the asterisked items in your boxes and note below which one of these four items is the #1 item to pay attention to *right now*—and why. What action would you want to take toward addressing your #1 item?

_____

_____

_____

_____

_____

# 4 The Stages of Change Model

*PURPOSE:* To identify your current readiness for change by applying the Stages of Change model to your own experience.

## DID YOU KNOW?

If you have weighed the pros and cons of your use, perhaps you have a better picture of your ongoing relationship with substances, both positive and negative. Are you ready for a change? Before you decide, let's look first at how people typically make changes. The Stages of Change model, developed by psychologists James Prochaska, Carlo DiClemente, and John Norcross (1992), is a wonderful tool that can be used not just to identify where you are with your motivation to stop using substances, but for all kinds of life decisions, such as leaving relationships, changing jobs, losing weight, and so on. For our purposes, though, we'll stick to substance use.

You might have tried and failed before to cut back on or eliminate your substance use. That is normal and understandable. Most people don't just wake up one morning and say, "Okay, that's it! I've had enough," and put down their paraphernalia and never use again. Change is a process that typically follows these stages:

- **Precontemplation.** This is the stage when people are not thinking about changing their behavior. They are perfectly happy to continue using and are not especially concerned at the moment about any harmful consequences. Loved ones, friends, or healthcare professionals might have expressed concern, but people in the precontemplation stage of change don't believe they have a problem, at least not one that requires changing their habits.

- **Contemplation.** In this stage, people recognize that they have a problem with substance use and are thinking about the pros and cons of their use—the benefits and costs. They might also be thinking about cutting back or quitting *someday* but aren't doing anything about it right now.

- **Preparation.** People in this stage are starting to make small changes in their behavior. Perhaps they're cutting back on their use, or maybe setting a date in the future when they will quit or seek help, go to an AA meeting, get a physical exam, or check themselves into a treatment program.

- **Action.** In this stage, people are taking definite action toward changing their behavior, such as quitting outright, entering a detox or rehab facility, or attending an Alcoholics Anonymous (AA), Cocaine Anonymous (CA), Marijuana Anonymous (MA), or Narcotics Anonymous (NA) meeting.

- **Maintenance.** The maintenance stage means that people have stopped using and have continued to abstain from substance use for around six months. While it is possible for people to maintain abstinence on their own, it is recommended that they join a support group, continue to ask for help, and build a solid, dependable safety network of supportive people to keep moving forward. We'll talk more about that later in this book.

- **Relapse.** Relapse is common, but it is not inevitable; still, because it does happen so much, it can be helpful to think of it as another stage of change. It can be devastating to break a period of abstinence with a return to use, but that doesn't mean all is lost. Addiction recovery can take many tries; it's also true that every day offers an opportunity to start over—and usually people who have been working on their substance-related problems can jump right back into the preparation or action stages of change without as much suffering as before.

- **Cycling.** *Cycling* refers to a pattern among many people in recovery when they go through the stages of change—from precontemplation to contemplation to preparation to action—and then experience continual slips and relapses without reaching the maintenance stage of about six months' abstinence. This is a frustrating pattern both for users and their loved ones. Working with an experienced addictions specialist can be vital for people who "cycle" so they can dig deeply into the internal and external circumstances that might be leading to continued use.

# DOES THIS SOUND LIKE YOU?

Can you relate to some of the stages of change described above? Do you have a sense of which stage you're currently in, and where you might like to be in the future? Be aware that you might be in different stages of change for different substances. That is, you might have quit using opiates (action/maintenance) but you're smoking marijuana and are not concerned about that (precontemplation). Let's look at each stage more closely using a series of brief vignettes.

## Precontemplation

*Robert, 23, is an unemployed college grad who lives with his parents and smokes marijuana daily, usually at a friend's house, where they hang out and play video games. He participates in a weekly substance-use group because his parents told him he should stop smoking. "I'm here because my parents said they'd cut off my allowance and take my phone away if I didn't show up," Robert says. "I doubt I'll ever stop smoking. I've always had anxiety, and this is the best thing for me. Nothing else works as well as weed, so I don't see what the problem is. I can't wait to move out and be on my own."*

Robert is in the precontemplation stage of change. Despite the threat of losing his allowance and phone, he is not ready to confront his addictive behaviors. The threat is serving as motivation from outside himself that isn't matched by motivation from within.

## Contemplation

*Vikram, 32, is a married, full-time graduate student working toward his master's degree in public health administration. He has been using nonprescription Adderall since he was a teenager. While he doesn't use it every day, he has begun to notice that he "can't do without it" when he needs to finish a paper or study for an exam. He now has high blood pressure and has lost some weight. Vikram's husband complains that Vikram is "always wired" and gets angry at him about his Adderall use, which he tries to hide, unsuccessfully. Vikram thinks it might be time to make a change. He tells his husband, "Maybe after final exams are over or maybe next year, when I get my degree, then I'll go to a doctor and see if there's something else they can recommend."*

Vikram is in the contemplation stage of change. He acknowledges there is a problem and is already experiencing some negative consequences of his ongoing use, but he is not yet ready to do anything about it. The contemplation stage of change can be identified as the "maybe someday" stage, which can last for years, even decades, or forever.

## Preparation

*Charlene, 35, is a married teacher and mother of two young children. Her husband recommended she seek treatment for her problem drinking. She drinks wine every night and then falls asleep, leaving him to manage the children's bedtime. She has agreed to go to therapy because she has noticed that she has been drinking more and more wine at night to "take the edge off," and part of her feels "ashamed" and "out of control." Charlene is sad at the thought of stopping, but she is motivated to do something about it. She decides to try "controlled drinking" for a few weeks, limiting herself to just one glass per night and no alcohol on weekends. "Then, maybe I'll quit on New Year's Day," she says.*

Charlene is in the preparation stage. She has mixed feelings about her use, is making small changes, but is not experiencing sufficient negative consequences to quit outright. Instead, she sets a "quit date." People in the preparation stage often find it helpful to set some limits and deadlines and check in with how that feels along the way. And this makes sense; it's a good feeling to make an actual plan, which is different from that "someday" syndrome.

## Action

*Leonard, a guitarist in a rock band, is approaching his thirtieth birthday. Leonard has been smoking marijuana several times a week for about twelve years, ever since he left home for college. His childhood friends have good jobs. Some are in long-term relationships, some have children, but Leonard feels like he isn't really progressing in life. So Leonard decides to quit smoking marijuana on his birthday, which, to him, is symbolic of becoming an adult. He tells his friends and his bandmates. He gets rid of his stash, his bongs, and his rolling papers. On his birthday, he throws himself a party at a restaurant and invites all his friends and family to celebrate this new beginning.*

Leonard is in the action stage—having gone through the precontemplation, contemplation, and preparation stages, he set a date and stuck to it. "It's not always easy," he says. He misses some of his old friends, but he feels better about himself and is happy to be moving forward in a positive way, taking responsibility, and making healthier choices.

## Maintenance

*Keisha, 58, had been dependent on alcohol for many years. Her wife, Daphne, and their children had confronted her about her problem a few years back, and she thought maybe she did have a problem. After numerous cycles of detox, rehab, outpatient treatment, and AA meetings, she still felt guilty, ashamed, and out of control, which would lead her to pick up again. When her doctor told her she was at risk for liver disease and other chronic health problems, Keisha went to another program, and this time she "got it"—in her words, "Life is short. I'm almost sixty. I don't want to die young like my mother, who drank herself to death." Keisha completed the program and immediately became involved with her local LGBTQ+-friendly AA meetings. She hasn't had a drink in nearly a year.*

Keisha is in the maintenance stage—she is highly motivated and has a good support network and good sobriety skills. She says it's a challenge sometimes, but she feels better about herself and hopeful about her future, physically, emotionally, and spiritually.

## Relapse

*Sarra, 35, was known as a "party girl" throughout her twenties and early thirties—both as a user and an occasional dealer of cocaine. For some years, she was able to maintain the lifestyle and hold down a high-pressure job as a real-estate agent. Eventually, the effects of long-term coke use led to damage in her nasal passage, which required surgery to repair. Sarra declared she was "done forever" with coke. She left her job to find a more stable income as a sales rep and became active in Cocaine Anonymous. She worked the 12 steps and, for a year or so, felt happier than she had ever recalled being. Then her beloved brother died suddenly in a car accident. Sarra began isolating more and fantasized constantly about getting high. Sarra impulsively called her old dealer one day, and they snorted "just one line for old time's sake." One line led to another, and soon she was in a full-blown relapse for several months.*

Sarra's story is an example of the relapse stage of this model—despite a long period of sobriety and many lifestyle changes, Sarra remained vulnerable to her addiction in the face of sudden loss and trauma. After this relapse, Sarra shored up her support system, deleted her dealer's number, and got back to work on the 12 steps, determined to get back to recovery—one day at a time.

## Cycling

*Dennis, 30, has been using opiates for nearly a decade. His use began following surgery for a sports injury. In the past two years, he has graduated to intravenous heroin use. Dennis has been in several inpatient and day programs and has had short periods of abstinence, but then goes back to using. He has overdosed twice already, requiring resuscitation with Narcan. While he acknowledges that those near-death experiences are a problem, he says he's not ruling out using again. Dennis attends groups and NA meetings and has started seeing a psychiatrist for Suboxone, a medication to treat opiate dependence. He starts to feel better but then misses the high, so sometimes he skips taking the medication for a couple of days and uses heroin. His doctor advises that he is not yet on a solid maintenance dose of Suboxone, which will help greatly with cravings. "I know I'm in trouble. But I don't want to have the 'crutch' of a pill. I want to do it on my own," Dennis says.*

Dennis is caught in a repeating cycle of using, not using, using, not using. Despite having a compassionate doctor and therapist who understand the physical and emotional challenges of recovering from long-term opiate addiction, Dennis remains ambivalent about using Suboxone, perhaps because he perceives some cultural stigma about using medication. His family is at their wits' end, and they don't know how they can help him "until he is ready to help himself." They are worried the doctor will terminate the prescription if Dennis doesn't take the medication as prescribed.

If you relapse or are in a period of cycling, remember, it's not the end of the world. You can start back on the path to recovery right away with self-compassion and the willingness to ask for help. It doesn't matter how many times you have relapsed and how many times you start over again—*every attempt at sobriety is worthy of celebration.* Keep going. Believe it or not, you can go from relapse to the action stage of change in a matter of hours and, with help and hope, work toward maintaining those changes.

# WHAT TO DO

In this exercise, reflect on your own stage of change, being as honest as you can be.

What stage of change best describes where you are *right now* in your process? Explain why you chose that stage.

_____

_____

_____

_____

_____

_____

Think of a time (now or in the past) when you were in the precontemplation stage, whether with substances or another habit or life decision. Describe when and where, and what it was like.

_____

_____

_____

_____

What about the contemplation stage? Describe when and where, and what it was like.

_____

_____

_____

_____

What about the preparation stage? Describe when and where, and what it was like.

_____

_____

_____

_____

Have you ever been in the action stage of change? Describe when and where, and what it was like.

_____

_____

_____

_____

_____

Describe any time when you have been in the maintenance stage—that is, maintained your desired change—for at least six months.

_____

_____

_____

_____

_____

Describe any time when you moved from the action stage into relapse or cycling. What happened next?

_____

_____

_____

_____

_____

# 5   Dear Self...Yes, You! Part I

*PURPOSE:* To build self-empowerment and prevent relapse by beginning a dialogue with the different parts of yourself.

## DID YOU KNOW?

Throughout this workbook, you'll have opportunities to build a new, healthier relationship with yourself. You can learn to notice your inner dialogue. When you're starting to recover from drug and alcohol use, it can often turn nasty and critical and then sabotage your progress. You might think the answer is to get rid of that voice. Quite the contrary. That critical voice isn't your enemy— it's your teacher! Developing a consistent, compassionate dialogue with yourself can be vital to maintaining long-term sobriety.

## DOES THIS SOUND LIKE YOU?

*Mack, 35, says he has an "intimate relationship" with the angel and devil on his shoulders that talk noisily to him all the time about his excessive use of the painkiller Vicodin: "Come on, you can take one! What difference will it make?" or "Who's going to know? It'll help you relax." Then the other voice kicks in: "You know you can't stop at one pill. Once you start, you'll want another, and another," or "Remember what happened last time? You ended up missing work the next day!"*

How are you like Mack? How are you different?

_____

_____

_____

Does Mack's awareness of his two inner voices help or hurt his progress? Tell why.

_____

_____

_____

## WHAT TO DO

In this exercise, you'll first identify two specific inner voices—what we'll call your *wise self* and your *addicted self*—without attaching any judgment to either of those labels. Some call them the "angel" and the "devil" sitting on their shoulders. Your *wise self* is the one who knows the negative consequences of using drugs and alcohol and is determined to do something about it. Your *addicted self* is the one who, despite the negative consequences, continues to use substances.

On the following lines, write down some of the familiar phrases that come to mind when you pay attention to what your *wise self* has to say.

Examples:

- "I know it's hard and you've tried to stop drinking before. Let's give it another chance."

- "Using heroin doesn't mean you're a loser. You are a good person."

- "It's okay to ask for help."

- "You'll feel better when you're not thinking about smoking weed all the time."

You might want to look back at "Weighing Your Pros and Cons—with a Twist" (exercise 3), where you identified what you see as the benefits and costs of using and not using substances.

_____

_____

_____

_____

_____

Next, write down some of the familiar phrases that come to mind when you pay attention to what your *addicted self* has to say.

Examples:

- "I don't care anymore. I just want to get high."

- "Leave me alone. I'm a lost cause."

- "You don't understand. I need to get drunk."

- "I can't change, no matter how hard I try."

_____

_____

_____

_____

_____

Now, try to bring the two voices together by writing a short letter from your wise self to your addicted self. Use extra paper if needed. What wisdom does your wise self want to offer your addicted self? How can your wise self listen to and be more patient with your addicted self?

Don't worry if you don't feel very wise right now. That can develop over time. Just do your best. If you have a hard time accessing a wise voice, think about what a wise person you admire might say to your addicted self, the self who is courageous enough to ask for help.

Dear Addicted Self,

_____

_____

_____

_____

_____

_____

_____

_____

_____

_____

_____

_____

_____

_____

_____

_____

_____

We will return to this exercise later in the workbook so you can see how these voices have developed over time.

# Know Your Triggers

# 6  What Are Your Triggers?

*PURPOSE:* To make more positive choices and avoid unwanted slips by learning what your triggers are.

## DID YOU KNOW?

You might have heard the term *trigger* before, especially if you've tried quitting or cutting back on drug or alcohol use in the past. A trigger can be a person, place, or object (external triggers); a memory, emotion, or sensation (internal triggers); or a situation (internal or external) that makes you think about using and that might cause you to pick up.

Triggers can often seem to have a life of their own, controlling your moods and behaviors, outside of your conscious awareness: "…and the next thing I knew, I was at the liquor store [or calling my dealer]." Knowing your personal triggers is key to self-awareness. And self-awareness is key to your recovery!

## DOES THIS SOUND LIKE YOU?

*Angela, 31, is nine weeks abstinent from alcohol. She nearly lost her job as a result of chronic alcohol-related absences. Her employer referred her to an employee assistance program, and she attended a thirty-day residential program, followed by a two-week day treatment program. She now sees an individual therapist and attends AA meetings four times a week. She has daily urges and finds herself thinking about alcohol a lot. Angela is making some sober friends, but 90 percent of the people in her social network drink, and some never knew about her problem. At a friend's wedding shower, Angela thinks she's "strong enough" to resist drinking, but once the mimosas are passed around and everyone's laughing, Angela starts to feel sad and angry. She wishes she, too, could drink in moderation, "like a normal person." On some level, she also resents that the host, who is aware she's in early recovery and had expressed support for Angela's sobriety, decided to serve alcohol at all.*

How are you like Angela? How are you different?

_____

_____

_____

What were Angela's external triggers in this situation? Her internal triggers?

_____

_____

_____

# WHAT TO DO

In this exercise, you'll identify your personal triggers. As with all the exercises in this book, be as honest and nonjudgmental as you can as you make your lists. Don't hold back. Once you know your triggers, you can make more positive choices and avoid an unwanted slip or relapse.

List the people in your life with whom you might use alcohol or drugs:

_____

_____

_____

_____

List the people in your life who are possible triggers to your picking up alcohol or drugs, besides the people you are likely to use with:

_____

_____

_____

_____

List the places where you might be likely to use alcohol or drugs:

_____

_____

_____

_____

List the time(s) of day when you might be likely to use alcohol or drugs:

_____

_____

_____

_____

List any objects (paraphernalia, books, magazines, ATM, phone, and so on) you might encounter that might trigger you to want to use alcohol or drugs:

_____

_____

_____

_____

List any specific memories or experiences (a certain song, a romantic encounter, a traumatic event, a loss) that are likely to trigger your desire to use:

_____

_____

_____

_____

List any emotions (anger, sadness, fear, anxiety, depression, jealousy, shame, loneliness, happiness, excitement, and so on) you're aware of that might trigger you to use. These can be positive or negative emotions:

_____

_____

_____

_____

List any physical sensations (aches, withdrawal symptoms, cold or flu, pain) that might trigger you to use:

_____

_____

_____

_____

List specific situations (family gathering, party, holidays, work meeting, sports event, job interview, going on a date) that might trigger you to use:

_____

_____

_____

_____

Now, notice, *with compassion and without judgment,* the difference between your internal and external triggers. Are your internal or your external triggers more likely to cause you to use substances, or are they about equal? Write a few notes here about what you notice. If you are seeing a therapist, you might want to bring what you've written in this exercise to a session.

_____

_____

_____

_____

With increased awareness and a mindset of curiosity and self-compassion, you can learn to recognize and better manage your triggers. You may want to come back to this exercise as you progress and notice how your relationship to your triggers changes over time.

# 7  Noticing Your Urges and Cravings

*PURPOSE:* To gain better control by recognizing and tracking your urges and cravings.

## DID YOU KNOW?

Now that you are more familiar with what people, places, and things might trigger your desire to use substances, let's look more closely at that desire to use, or what are called *urges and cravings.*

Urges and cravings—terms that are often used interchangeably—are a challenging part of recovery, especially in the early stages. Most people would describe an urge or craving as a powerful physical sensation or mental compulsion to use their substance of choice. Physical urges and cravings are frequently accompanied by a sudden stream of thoughts that make you feel compelled to pick up, as if there is no choice. People who are not in recovery from drug and alcohol use might relate by recalling a time when they were "dying for" that first cup of coffee in the morning or a sugary treat after dinner.

Books and articles about addiction often point to the role of "positive" hormones—such as endorphins and dopamine, which can cause euphoric feelings—in feeding the cycle of addiction. We won't be delving into brain chemistry here, but you should know that the feeling of being out of control and helpless in the face of a craving can in large part be chemically based, especially for people who've been using substances for a long time.

Once you get better at identifying your triggers, which often lead to urges and cravings, you can take steps to feel more in control.

## DOES THIS SOUND LIKE YOU?

*Roderigo, 19, had been using prescription Xanax, a benzodiazepine, to treat his anxiety for two years. He wanted to stop using Xanax because he was afraid he was addicted and wanted to face his life stresses without medication. His doctor put him on a slow program to taper off, and now Roderigo hasn't used any benzodiazepines for the past month. At random times throughout the day, Roderigo also has some mild shakiness and a fluttering heart. "It freaks me out," he says, "because I can't tell what's anxiety and what the doctor thinks might be chemical withdrawal symptoms." He describes both a strong physical craving for the Xanax and difficulty letting go of his obsessive thoughts about wanting to take a pill.*

How are you like Roderigo? How are you different?

_____

_____

_____

Have you experienced physical or mental urges or cravings for your substance of choice? Describe them briefly.

_____

_____

_____

_____

_____

_____

## WHAT TO DO

For the next several weeks, notice and record, or be mindful of, your urges or cravings: when they occur, where you are and whether you are alone, how intense they are on a scale from 1 to 10 (1 = mild, 5 = moderate, 10 = intense), and how long they last. As you do this exercise, remember to do your best to let go of any judgment, shame, or guilt, and just notice.

| Example | Time of day | Where were you? Alone or with others? | How intense was it? | How long did it last? |
| --- | --- | --- | --- | --- |
| Tuesday | 8 p.m. | Home alone unexpectedly | 7 | 10 minutes |

Week of _____

| Day | Time of day | Where were you? Alone or with others? | How intense was it? | How long did it last? |
|---|---|---|---|---|
| Sunday | | | | |
| Monday | | | | |
| Tuesday | | | | |
| Wednesday | | | | |
| Thursday | | | | |
| Friday | | | | |
| Saturday | | | | |

If you find this exercise helpful, or you want to experiment with it on an ongoing basis, you can find a downloadable version of this worksheet at http://www.newharbinger.com/52762.

Now that you've begun to notice the people, places, and things that trigger you and the frequency and duration of your urges and cravings, what can you do? Here are some options:

- Stop. Breathe. Feel your feet on the ground. Count to ten. Keep breathing.

- Distract yourself by doing something else—read, write, walk, run, go to the gym, have a snack, play a video game. (See also exercise 10, "Alternatives to Using.")

- Call a safe person, someone who will help you avoid picking up without judging or shaming you.

- Go to an AA or SMART Recovery meeting.

- Practice "urge surfing," in which you simply notice the urge and its intensity, like a wave coming to shore. You don't have to do anything. Just watch the urge arrive, swell, peak, and then get smaller, until it disappears. Sometimes cravings last a few seconds, sometimes a few minutes or more. Most cravings diminish much more quickly than you'd think.

For this exercise, chart your responses to your urges and cravings over the next week, adding the information in the new column on the right.

| Example | Time of day | Where were you? Alone or with others? | How intense was it? | How long did it last? | What was your response? What was the result? |
|---------|-------------|---------------------------------------|---------------------|-----------------------|----------------------------------------------|
| Sunday | 1 p.m. | After an AA meeting | 7 | 5 minutes | Told a buddy that I was triggered. Talked through it. It helped. |

Week of_____

| Day | Time of day | Where were you? Alone or with others? | How intense was it? | How long did it last? | What was your response? What was the result? |
|---|---|---|---|---|---|
| Sunday | | | | | |
| Monday | | | | | |
| Tuesday | | | | | |
| Wednesday | | | | | |
| Thursday | | | | | |
| Friday | | | | | |
| Saturday | | | | | |

Again, if you would find it useful to track your responses to urges and cravings for a longer period, you can download a worksheet for this exercise at http://www.newharbinger.com/52762.

# 8  Reasons Not to Use

*PURPOSE:* To keep focused on your main reasons for wanting to stop using substances by creating a handy visual reminder.

## DID YOU KNOW?

Now that you're beginning to take charge of your life in a healthier way, it can sometimes feel overwhelming to make so many changes at once. One simple activity that helps people in early recovery is to identify their specific reasons for not using, and to keep that list (or another visual reminder) front and center at all times.

## DOES THIS SOUND LIKE YOU?

*Mario, 50, a lawyer and father of three, has relapsed so many times on a combination of alcohol and pills that he has lost count. Now, his wife has threatened to leave with the kids if he doesn't stop using. In addition, he hasn't been to the doctor in two years and worries that his liver might be affected by his substance use. Mario has to face up to the possibility that he could lose everything he really cares about: his job, his marriage, his kids, his health. In his head, he knows the main reasons he shouldn't use and what's at stake, but he always seems to forget those reasons and acts on impulse instead.*

How are you like Mario? How are you different?

_____

_____

_____

How do you feel about expressing your reasons for not using? Does it make you feel happy? Sad? Scared? Guilty? Describe briefly.

_____

_____

_____

# WHAT TO DO

First, make a list of all the reasons why you are choosing to work on your substance use right now. You might want to refer back to your vision statement (exercise 2) and "Weighing Your Pros and Cons—with a Twist" (exercise 3) for some ideas.

Examples:

- "My kids need me around."

- "I don't want to lose my marriage."

- "I want to regain my parents' trust."

- "I want to feel better about myself."

- "I don't want to die."

Here are a few general categories to start you thinking:

- Better physical health

- Better mental health (less depression, anxiety, and so on)

- Saving money

- Improving job or school performance

- Better relationship with spouse or significant other

- Better relationship with your children

- Better relationship with your parents and other family members

- Better relationships with friends and colleagues

- Your "wants" and vision for the future

- _____

- _____

- _____

- _____

- _____

- _____

- _____

- _____

Next, narrow your list of reasons down to your top six:

1. _____

2. _____

3. _____

4. _____

5. _____

6. _____

Now comes the fun part! Take your list and create an attractive, easily accessible way to look at it whenever you feel your motivation is down. You might want to write your list on an index card or colorful piece of paper and keep it in your wallet or purse. Or you can enter your list of reasons directly onto your smartphone, using the note function. Or, instead of a list, you can download positive images onto your phone or computer—photos of loved ones or other inspiring graphics to remind you of your main reasons not to use. You can even print your images out and create a bigger vision board that expresses what matters to you and that will keep you going in your recovery. Be creative!

Look at your list or your images as often as you need to—and feel free to edit or change your reasons as needed. As you continue to identify your internal and external triggers and tune in to when you have an urge or craving, you'll get better at noticing those thoughts and feelings.

# Take Action

# 9   Housecleaning

*PURPOSE:* To minimize your risk of relapse by taking specific steps to get rid of objects and avoid people and situations that might trigger you to use.

## DID YOU KNOW?

When you decide to stop using substances, it's important to take active steps to minimize your chances of relapse. *Access* to your substance of choice and the *opportunity* to use it are two key elements that can lead to a relapse or the temptation to relapse. Limiting access and opportunity are smart, healthy choices, but it might not be easy. As with everything in your recovery, be sure to ask for help and support from people you trust to honor your decision.

## DOES THIS SOUND LIKE YOU?

*Liza, 20, has been using nonprescription Percocet since she was seventeen. Her parents have sent her to multiple treatment programs, but whenever she moves back home, she relapses. Upon her return from a wilderness program, Liza's parents were worried. They gave her an ultimatum: "Thirty days of passing your drug tests or find a place of your own." Liza knew she'd stashed pills in different places around the house, including a few fentanyl pills she'd gotten from her boyfriend, Joshua. She worried that if she found one, she wouldn't be able to resist. On the recommendation of her counselor, she asked her parents to help her search the house to be sure all the pills were gone. They combed through closets and drawers, under the bed, under the mattress, and in clothes pockets. They found several long-forgotten, unused pills, which they disposed of together. It wasn't easy, and Liza had lots of mixed feelings. Part of her still craved opiates, but, ultimately, she told herself she was doing the best thing for her future.*

How are you like Liza? How are you different?

_____

_____

_____

Have you ever taken steps to limit your access and opportunity to use your substance of choice? How would you feel about doing what Liza did?

_____

_____

_____

_____

# WHAT TO DO

In this exercise, you'll work on moving from the contemplation stage of change, discussed in exercise 4, to the preparation and action stages. You'll take stock of your physical environment as well as your social network, think about your access to money, and make some tough choices about letting go of things and people who could interfere with your progress.

## Taking Stock of Your Environment

First, schedule a specific time to go through your home and get rid of items that put you at risk of using. Commit to it! Ask a trusted person to witness your activity, if you wish.

Date _____ Time _____

Next, go through your house or apartment and dispose of any and all of the following substances or paraphernalia. Don't forget to toss that last little pill or nip or joint or stash that you've hidden. Setting a little something aside just in case is sometimes called "reserving the right to use," and it's a setup for failure.

- Alcohol

- Ashtrays

- Bongs, pipes, etc.

- Lighters

- Marijuana

- Medical marijuana card

- Mirrors

- Needles, syringes, spoons, etc.

- Nonprescription pills

- Other abusable drugs, such as cough medicine

- Prescription pills you might abuse

- Rolling papers

- Vaping devices

If you live with someone who has access to or uses substances that put you at risk for picking up (for example, prescription drugs), buy a lockbox and have them keep those items in a secret, locked place.

## Limiting Access to Money

If you are at risk of picking up drugs or alcohol whenever you have some cash in your pocket, set up a system for yourself to limit access to money. Some people choose to get rid of their bank cards altogether or sign over their account to a loved one. Some arrange to have someone else give them an allowance and then keep track of any expenses together. "But I'm too old for that!" some might say, or "That makes me feel like a child again!"

If you are putting your recovery first, you might tell yourself this: "I'm doing this because I want to have a happier life. It doesn't matter what people think. I'm not reverting to childhood—in fact, I'm being smart. I'm acting like a mature, responsible adult by doing what I need to do to limit my chances of relapse."

Sound good? Great! Below, write down the exact steps you will take to limit your access to money, starting today. Include what people you need to notify, what bank accounts or other sources of income you want to restrict access to, and by what dates you want to accomplish these steps.

| Source of money | Action step | Person to notify (if applicable) | Date by which you will do this | How did it feel to take this step? |
|---|---|---|---|---|
| Liza's example: ATM card | Commit to no ATM use for three months. | Give card to Mom. | Today! | Scary but empowering, also sad. |
| | | | | |
| | | | | |
| | | | | |

## Taking Stock of Your Social Network

As you know, people in your social network can be triggers to using: for instance, family members, friends, and colleagues. Instead of waiting for a possible tempting situation, you can be proactive in support of your sobriety. Tell people in your social network that you are working hard to stay sober and that you don't want to be around anyone who is drinking or using drugs. Ask them not to invite you to events where drugs or alcohol might be present. Ask them not to discuss the "good old days" or refer to their recent binge or wild party. (See also "Say No," which appears in exercise 11.)

Along the way, you might encounter people who care about you but who just don't get how serious your situation is and who might push you to use "just this once." For your best chance at success, you might need to limit contact with these people, at least for the short term. Tell them directly about your decision in person, by phone, or text, or email—whatever is best for you. Ask them to respect your decision and give you the space you need to recover.

If this doesn't work—that is, if the person doesn't honor your request—you can:

• Delete their numbers from your phone.

• Block them from texting or calling.

- Block them on social media.

- Tell them in person or by email or text that you no longer want to have contact.

- Say no to social events that might put you in proximity to this person or otherwise trigger you to use.

*Example: Liza decided to text her boyfriend, Joshua, to say that she was back from rehab, determined to stay sober, and needed to break up. He texted right back, saying he was so happy for her and would love to see her just to celebrate, nothing more. She was torn but took a few deep breaths and said that wasn't a good idea. He promised he wouldn't try to get her to use. She said again it wasn't a good idea. He continued to press. Even though she was still torn, her desire to stop using (and to stay in her parents' house) outweighed her desire to see Joshua. She wished him well but said she would not be answering calls or texts for the foreseeable future.*

Add any other "housecleaning" items here that might be helpful in your recovery efforts:

_____

_____

_____

_____

# IO    Alternatives to Using

*PURPOSE:* To minimize the temptation to use by identifying pleasurable activities to do instead of turning to drugs or alcohol.

## DID YOU KNOW?

Another challenging part of starting on the road to sobriety can be figuring out what to do instead of using. Maybe you have a lot of time on your hands since you're not chasing down your dealer or planning your next high or battling a hangover. Or maybe you can't remember what you used to do before you ever started using.

Maybe using has been so much a part of your daily life that you haven't given a thought to what else could possibly give you pleasure. If any of the above examples strikes a chord, you're not alone. It's a normal and understandable part of recovery and nothing to be ashamed of.

But now, it's time to rejoin life—at your own pace, in your own time.

## DOES THIS SOUND LIKE YOU?

*Kit, 25, has been using cocaine recreationally since high school, first sniffing in the bathroom at school and then snorting lines in the back room at her waitressing job and after work. Her day often revolves around finding coke, getting high, crashing, and starting the cycle over again the next day. Recently, she had a series of panic attacks that scared her to death, so Kit decided to quit. She's proud of her decision and is dealing with some withdrawal symptoms, but after a week of not using, she told her best friend, "I'm so bored now! What do sober people actually do every day?"*

How are you like Kit? How are you different?

_____

_____

_____

What do you think a good starting point would be for Kit to find things to do besides using?

_____

_____

_____

How do you deal with boredom?

_____

_____

_____

# WHAT TO DO

Review the following list and put a checkmark next to at least *fifteen* activities that you would consider doing. Then write down which ones you'll commit to doing and in what time period. Be realistic, but don't play it 100 percent safe. Do something new! You might want to think about which activities will help you grow and learn, which ones would help you tackle any boredom that you might experience, and which would directly contribute to preventing a relapse. (See "A Note on Boredom," which appears in exercise 16.)

- [ ] Acting
- [ ] Arranging flowers
- [ ] Attending a prayer group
- [ ] Attending family get-togethers
- [ ] Bowling
- [ ] Building models
- [ ] Buying books
- [ ] Buying clothes
- [ ] Buying gifts
- [ ] Buying household gadgets
- [ ] Buying music
- [ ] Camping
- [ ] Canoeing
- [ ] Cleaning
- [ ] Collecting stamps
- [ ] Collecting things (coins, shells)
- [ ] Cooking

- [ ] Dancing
- [ ] Daydreaming
- [ ] Debating
- [ ] Discussing books
- [ ] Doing arts and crafts
- [ ] Doing karate or martial arts
- [ ] Doing needlepoint
- [ ] Doing yoga
- [ ] Doodling
- [ ] Dressing up and looking nice
- [ ] Driving
- [ ] Eating
- [ ] Enjoying a quiet evening
- [ ] Entertaining
- [ ] Exercising
- [ ] Fantasizing about the future
- [ ] Fishing
- [ ] Flying kites
- [ ] Gardening

- [ ] Getting a massage
- [ ] Going hang gliding
- [ ] Going horseback riding
- [ ] Going on a date
- [ ] Going on a picnic
- [ ] Going out to dinner
- [ ] Going to a baseball game or other sports event
- [ ] Going to a Meetup group
- [ ] Going to a museum
- [ ] Going to plays and concerts
- [ ] Going to religious services
- [ ] Going to the beach
- [ ] Going to the mountains
- [ ] Going to the movies
- [ ] Golfing
- [ ] Having lunch with a friend
- [ ] Having political discussions
- [ ] Having sex

- ☐ Hiking
- ☐ Jogging
- ☐ Kayaking
- ☐ Kissing
- ☐ Knitting
- ☐ Laughing
- ☐ Lighting candles
- ☐ Listening to music
- ☐ Listening to the radio
- ☐ Making a gift for someone
- ☐ Meditating
- ☐ Meeting new people
- ☐ Painting
- ☐ Planning my career
- ☐ Planning to go to school
- ☐ Playing a musical instrument
- ☐ Playing cards
- ☐ Playing soccer
- ☐ Playing softball
- ☐ Playing tennis or pickleball
- ☐ Playing volleyball
- ☐ Playing with pets or other animals
- ☐ Praying alone
- ☐ Reading a book
- ☐ Recalling happy moments in my childhood
- ☐ Recycling old items
- ☐ Refinishing furniture
- ☐ Reflecting on how I've improved
- ☐ Remembering words/deeds of loving people
- ☐ Repairing things around the house
- ☐ Riding a motorbike
- ☐ Running track
- ☐ Sailing
- ☐ Sewing
- ☐ Shooting pool
- ☐ Sightseeing
- ☐ Singing around the house
- ☐ Singing with groups
- ☐ Sitting in a sidewalk café
- ☐ Skating
- ☐ Skiing
- ☐ Sleeping
- ☐ Soaking in the bathtub
- ☐ Solving crossword puzzles
- ☐ Spending time with good friends
- ☐ Surfing
- ☐ Swimming
- ☐ Taking a college class
- ☐ Taking a sauna or steam bath
- ☐ Taking a vacation
- ☐ Taking an adult education class
- ☐ Taking care of my plants
- ☐ Taking children places
- ☐ Taking photographs
- ☐ Talking on the phone
- ☐ Teaching
- ☐ Thinking about becoming active in the community
- ☐ Thinking how it will be when I finish school
- ☐ Traveling abroad or in the United States
- ☐ Volunteering
- ☐ Walking in my neighborhood
- ☐ Walking in the woods or on the beach
- ☐ Watching boxing
- ☐ Watching my children play
- ☐ Watching TV
- ☐ Woodworking
- ☐ Working on my car
- ☐ Wrestling
- ☐ Writing books or poems
- ☐ Writing in a diary or journal
- ☐ Other:

  _____

- ☐ Other:

  _____

Now list the fifteen activities you chose and when you want to do them by. Over the next few weeks, record which activities you actually did and what it was like for you. Refer back to this list, and delete or add to it as needed. And have fun!

| Activity | Do by | When done? | What was it like? |
|---|---|---|---|
|  |  |  |  |
|  |  |  |  |
|  |  |  |  |
|  |  |  |  |
|  |  |  |  |
|  |  |  |  |
|  |  |  |  |
|  |  |  |  |
|  |  |  |  |
|  |  |  |  |
|  |  |  |  |
|  |  |  |  |
|  |  |  |  |
|  |  |  |  |

# II  Your PLAN for Social Events

*PURPOSE:* To lower the risk of relapse by planning how to manage social events where you might be triggered.

## DID YOU KNOW?

One of the hardest challenges in your recovery will be making smart choices about social events and celebrations where alcohol or drugs are likely to be around: birthday parties, office parties, anniversaries, weddings, bridal or baby showers, graduations, funerals, religious ceremonies, family holidays—you name it. Sometimes you might have to attend an office event or function, a conference or meeting, where alcohol is readily available and where many, if not most, people will be drinking.

Usually this challenge is hardest for those with a specific history of alcohol use, because alcohol is everywhere in our culture—and it's glorified. But those with problem drug use can also be triggered by exposure and access to alcohol.

Since you can't hide in a cave the rest of your life, what can you do about exposure to alcohol?

## DOES THIS SOUND LIKE YOU?

*Mei, 50, a divorced corporate executive who has ninety days' abstinence from alcohol, is asked by her company to give an in-person presentation at an out-of-town conference where there will be receptions, happy hours, and working meals. She will be traveling alone and knows only one other person from her company who will be there. In the past, Mei would stay in a hotel that had a minibar in each room. She worries that the whole event will trigger her to pick up.*

How are you like Mei? How are you different?

_____

_____

_____

Have you ever been confronted with a similar situation? What did you do?

_____

_____

_____

What do you think Mei can do to avoid using alcohol? Write some notes here.

_____

_____

_____

_____

# WHAT TO DO

This exercise will teach you the PLAN strategy for relapse prevention. PLAN stands for

**P**repare

**L**isten

**A**cknowledge

Say **N**o

Most experts agree that the safest thing to do if you are triggered by the sight, smell, and general availability of alcohol is to avoid the event altogether. This is always a choice. But sometimes you really don't want to have to miss the wedding of a loved one or dear friend, or you might be in a situation, like Mei's, when not going to an event might lead to other negative consequences. Use PLAN to help you manage these unavoidable situations.

## Prepare

At least a few weeks before you attend this event, do some research. Find out as much as you can about what you might encounter so you won't be surprised and so you can be prepared with an "escape route" if necessary. Leave nothing to chance.

Event _____ Date _____

Time of day _____ Expected length of event _____

Location _____

List all the people you know who will be at the event:

_____

_____

_____

Of those people, does anyone know about your decision not to drink or use drugs? Who?

_____

Identify at least one person from the above list who can be your "buddy" at the event.

If no one will be available at the event itself, identify a "buddy" you can call or text (friend, spouse, sponsor, someone supportive).

Buddy's name _____ Phone number _____

Arrange in advance to check in with your buddy at least once during the event, *even if you feel you're in a good place.* You might be wondering, *Why would I need to reach out if I'm feeling confident?* Because in early recovery, it's important to practice the habit of staying connected with others and setting up go-to ways to be accountable. The more you practice these skills, the more solid your sobriety can become.

Find out if there will be an open bar: (Y/N) _____ Cash bar? (Y/N)_____

If yes, what can you order for yourself instead of alcohol? Many people choose seltzer with lime, juice, soda, and so on.

_____

The more you think about these things in advance, the better chance you have not to do something impulsive. Tell everyone you feel comfortable telling not to offer you alcohol!

## Listen

Part of starting sober today includes listening to your wise self and your addicted self, discussed in exercise 5, in advance of an event. Is your wise self telling you that going to this event is a smart or not-so-smart choice? Is your addicted self excited about the possibility of using? Listen closely to your inner voices without judgment or criticism. Write down what your wise self and your addicted self are saying when you think about going to this event. Remember to be honest with and compassionate toward yourself.

_____

_____

_____

_____

_____

_____

## Acknowledge

Even if you really want to go or absolutely must go to this event, what are your fears and worries, hopes and expectations? Can you acknowledge what risks you might be taking and strengthen your PLAN to minimize the risk of relapse? Write down your thoughts here, being as honest as you can. And remember, there is no "right" answer; everything you're thinking and feeling is okay to think and feel.

_____

_____

_____

_____

_____

_____

_____

## Say No

Again, it's always an option to decline an invitation to an event. In recovery, *you get to do what's best for you,* even if other people pressure you or criticize you. That's called healthy selfishness, and it's especially useful for people pleasers or those who have a hard time saying no in general.

Assess whether you have prepared for an event enough to be able to say no at, say, an open or cash bar, or to people passing around a joint or doing lines in the bathroom. (One client once reported that a relative was passing around Xanax at a *funeral.*) If you feel you are at risk, say no to the invitation, send your regrets, and perhaps arrange to visit those people at a later time.

If you do decide to go, practice some ways to say no to an offer of alcohol and/or drugs. For example:

- "No, thanks." (Simple, succinct, move on.) Or, after saying, "No, thanks," add:

- "I'm good."

- "I don't drink/smoke/use drugs."

- "I don't like the taste of alcohol."

- "I'm allergic."

- "I'm on a diet and avoiding alcohol."

- "I've had a problem with drinking/using drugs in the past."

- (Fill in your own)_____

- (Fill in your own) _____

After the event, write down your experience on the lines below, and make note of what you said or did to prevent yourself from picking up. If you did slip and pick up, write about that in detail so you can refer to it at a later date.

_____

_____

_____

_____

_____

_____

Follow-up: *Mei decided to stay at an Airbnb a short distance from the conference center, because she acknowledged that being in a hotel room with a mini-bar would be too strong a trigger. She arranged to call her AA sponsor every morning and text her best friend every evening—and they agreed that she could contact them any other time. She planned to chart any urges and cravings. Her plan also included not attending happy hour, ordering seltzer with lime at meals, and reviewing her "Reasons Not to Use" (exercise 8) twice a day. Since Mei was already practiced at saying no to offers of alcohol, she felt confident as she departed for the conference. Mei returned home having not picked up and reported that thinking through the PLAN strategy in advance had been very helpful.*

Mei had a great outcome following the PLAN. Remember, however, that slips or relapses, if they happen, are not the end of the world. The more you prepare for attending social events, the higher your chance of success at sobriety.

# Build a Safety Net

# I2  Creating a Safe Network

*PURPOSE:* To boost your chances of success by creating a list of people you can trust to be supportive.

## DID YOU KNOW?

Connecting with supportive people who will help you succeed with your recovery goals is an important part of your sobriety journey. Why? Simple answer: It's too hard to do alone! That's why it's important to start building and maintaining a safe network among all the people you know—family, friends, coworkers, fellow students, and community members.

If you join a self-help group such as AA or SMART Recovery or attend group therapy or counseling, you'll have lots of choices of people who will "get" you and understand what you're going through without judging or shaming you. Some of them might even become a sponsor or recovery buddy—someone very reliable who you can call 24/7 and who will be available to focus exclusively on you. You deserve to have as many people in this network as possible so that you have lots of options in case you hit a rough or vulnerable patch.

## DOES THIS SOUND LIKE YOU?

*Alexander, 27, is new to addiction recovery. He had become dependent on painkillers following back surgery two years ago. When his doctors, concerned about possible abuse, stopped writing him prescriptions, he ended up finding pills through a friend, or he ordered them from the internet. He also stole some from his mother's medicine chest. Alexander saw a show about addiction and realized he had a chemical dependency. After a stay at rehab, he feels better, but he knows he has nothing in place to continue his progress now that he is home. He doesn't want to go to AA or NA—"They're not for me," he says. "I'm not into all that spiritual stuff, and I'd rather not spill my guts to total strangers." Only a few people know about his history. He doesn't like to talk about it; he'd rather just figure it out alone.*

How are you like Alexander? How are you different?

_____

_____

_____

Do you tend to isolate? Do you feel worried or ashamed about telling people you are in recovery? Why or why not?

_____

_____

_____

_____

_____

_____

## WHAT TO DO

In this exercise, you'll begin to identify people who might be available to join your safe network as you become more comfortable asking for help and isolating yourself less. Do the best you can to choose people who are going to be supportive while helping you maintain the boundaries around substance use you wish to set—that is, supportive without being enabling. An *enabler* is usually someone who cares about you but might feed into your addictive behaviors by lending you money, driving you to meet your dealer, giving you "just one" drink to help you relax, and so on.

Before you begin, think about the qualities you would find helpful in a friend or loved one, such as kindness, acceptance, warmth, respectfulness, patience, and honesty. Does that person ever use drugs or alcohol? Would someone who uses substances be a safe person for you? Try to name three people in each category.

If you can't think of anyone off the top of your head, think about people who *might* be available to you, if you were to ask.

People in my family:

_____ Contact info: _____

_____ Contact info: _____

_____ Contact info: _____

People in my circle of friends:

_____ Contact info: _____

_____ Contact info: _____

_____ Contact info: _____

People at school or at my job:

_____ Contact info: _____

_____ Contact info: _____

_____ Contact info: _____

People in my community (AA or NA members, neighbors, clergy, religious community, fellow volunteers):

_____ Contact info: _____

_____ Contact info: _____

_____ Contact info: _____

Others:

_____ Contact info: _____

_____ Contact info: _____

_____ Contact info: _____

Next, set yourself a goal of reaching out to at least one person from each category—and give yourself a deadline for achieving that goal:

Family member:_____ By when? _____

Friend:_____ By when? _____

Someone at school or work: _____ By when? _____

Someone in my community: _____ By when? _____

Other: _____ By when? _____

## What to Say

Reaching out to someone, especially someone you don't know well, can be challenging for most of us. But building a safe network to support your sobriety will require stretching out of your comfort zone sometimes (see exercise 15). You might be surprised to find that many people love to be supportive of others and will be flattered that you asked!

Here are some ideas about what to say to the people on the list you've just created:

"Hi, do you have a minute? I have an important question I want to run by you."

"Hi, as you know, I'm working on stopping [drinking/using drugs], and I'm creating a list of people who would be willing to be available to support me along the way."

"Hi, I have a special favor I want to ask you. I am trying to connect with other people who aren't drinking or using drugs, and I wondered if you might join my network. Maybe I could call on you for support every now and then. Would that work for you?"

Below, write down some other phrases you might use to invite someone to be in your network:

_____

_____

_____

_____

_____

_____

In exercise 13, you'll see some specific ideas for how to ask for direct help from someone in your newly formed network.

# $I3$  Asking for Help

*PURPOSE:* To support your path to sobriety by learning and practicing more strategies for reaching out to others for help and support, especially if you are usually the helper.

## DID YOU KNOW?

In the previous exercise, you made a list of people who could be available if you need help in your recovery or in life in general, and you set a deadline by which you'd ask them to join your safe, sober network. You wrote down some ideas about what you might say to those people. Great job!

Now let's tackle a problem a lot of people in recovery have faced—and have stumbled over—throughout their lives: how to take action to ask for help. Sometimes it's easier said than done.

Again, it's common among people with substance-use histories to try to "disappear" or isolate—perhaps because of guilt, shame, or a sense of unworthiness; perhaps because they were abused or neglected as children; or perhaps because they were betrayed by a loved one and don't trust that anyone would want to help them. If those experiences are a part of your history, it is essential that you seek individual counseling or therapy to fully understand and ultimately come to terms with those hurts and traumas.

For now, know that no matter your history, you deserve help and support. You deserve not to carry the weight of the world on your shoulders or take care of everyone else's needs before your own. If you go to enough AA meetings or other support groups, you'll likely learn that "people pleaser" is a common label among people in recovery. People also find the 12 steps of AA helpful in understanding the cost (and benefit, too) of taking care of others' needs.

## DOES THIS SOUND LIKE YOU?

*Yasmin, 43, is a single mother of two teenagers who works part time as an office manager. She is in early recovery from a combination of drug and alcohol use. Before entering treatment, Yasmin felt responsible for doing all the driving, cooking, cleaning, and household tasks, and she was very resentful and burned out: "I have to take care of everyone else, and I always put myself last." Yasmin realizes she needs to change but isn't sure how to go about setting limits or getting help.*

How are you like Yasmin? How are you different?

_____

_____

_____

What is one step Yasmin could take to start practicing getting help?

_____

_____

_____

_____

## WHAT TO DO

In this exercise, you'll first reflect on times in your life when you've asked for help—from simple things like asking someone to help you do a household task to asking for a ride to the airport to asking someone to watch the kids while you take time for yourself. List three of those times on the lines below.

1. _____

_____

_____

_____

2. _____

_____

_____

_____

3. _____

_____

_____

_____

Now, write down three times in your life when you really needed help and didn't ask anyone. Note when it happened (year or your age), who was involved, the reasons why you didn't ask (if you can recall), and what you remember feeling at the time.

1._____

_____

_____

_____

2._____

_____

_____

_____

3._____

_____

_____

_____

Now look at your list of people in your safe network from the previous exercise. Think about how each (or a few) of them might help you with something that you might need right now.

Here are some typical things that people who are people pleasers have difficulty asking for help with:

- Babysitting

- Being available by phone or text to check in during the day/evening

- Cooking a meal

- Getting a ride to a meeting or appointment

- Household chores

- Meeting in person for emotional support or encouragement

- Pet sitting

- Running an errand

- Talking on the phone for emotional support or encouragement

Now fill in your own ideas for tasks or other things you might need help with:

_____

_____

_____

_____

Record over the next week ways in which you need to, or could try to, ask for help.
Here are some ideas of how you might ask for help, by text, phone, email, or in person:

"Hi, _____. I'm wondering if you can help me with something."

"Hi, _____. I have a doctor's appointment on Tuesday at 3:00, and my car is in the shop. Would you be available and willing to drive me?"

"Hi, _____. I have to go to court for my DUI next week. I don't want my spouse to go because they're still too angry. Can you free up the time to come with me?"

"Hi, Mom. You know how I love your chocolate chip cookies? I really need some comfort food right now. Would you have time to bake a batch and bring them over?"

"Hi, _____. Are you going to the 7:00 meeting? Would you be able to pick me up? I'll chip in for gas, if that works for you."

You get the idea. Ask politely, assuming they have busy schedules. Be sure to say thank you. Someday, perhaps you'll be in a place where you can return the favor, but for now, you are the one who deserves to ask for help from friends and loving supporters along the way.

For the next week or so, record any situations when you need help, whom you asked and in what way, what you said, and what the outcome was. Even if you don't *really* need help, practice asking anyway and see what happens.

| Date | Needed help with... | Person asked? How contacted? What you said? | Outcome | Comments |
|------|---------------------|---------------------------------------------|---------|----------|
|      |                     |                                             |         |          |
|      |                     |                                             |         |          |
|      |                     |                                             |         |          |
|      |                     |                                             |         |          |

# I4 Tracking Your Recovery Activities

*PURPOSE:* To create accountability for your choices and actions by keeping track of your recovery-related activities.

## DID YOU KNOW?

One key ingredient of a sober life is staying active and accountable in your recovery. That means not leaving anything to chance. Even the people most motivated to break free from addiction will lose their momentum and determination at times or find themselves faced with challenges or setbacks they haven't anticipated. If you wait until one of those times, you might be too tired or burned out or anxious or depressed to reach out and ask for help if you are triggered to use.

Many experts believe that remaining engaged in *regular recovery-related activities* lowers your risk of slipping or relapsing. That's what we'll focus on in this exercise.

## DOES THIS SOUND LIKE YOU?

*Carolina, 36, juggles a full-time job as a college professor. She tries her best to join her wife and their three-year-old son for dinner each night, but she often has student conferences or faculty meetings. Carolina had been using cocaine recreationally for ten years before meeting her wife, then continued to use it occasionally in secret. She stopped when she got pregnant and became so busy that she rarely thought about using. After several recent office parties where a colleague put out lines of cocaine, however, she's been fantasizing about it a lot. She's never been in any kind of therapy and says she has no time for meetings or groups, nor is she friends with anyone who is in recovery.*

How are you like Carolina? How are you different?

_____

_____

_____

Do you think Carolina is at risk for abusing cocaine again? Why or why not? Write down your thoughts here and connect them to your own situation.

_____

_____

_____

_____

# WHAT TO DO

Perhaps you agree that Carolina could benefit from adding some recovery-related activities to her schedule, even if they add temporary stress to her life. In this exercise, you'll keep track of your recovery-related activities, meaning *specific events or actions that are directly related to your recovery from drug or alcohol use.* Later in this workbook, you'll read about other activities, such as physical exercise and meditation, which are essential tools for successful recovery as well.

Some recovery-related activities include:

- AA meeting

- MA meeting

- CA meeting

- NA meeting

- SMART Recovery meeting

- Inpatient program or rehab

- Meeting with sponsor or "recovery buddy"

- Intensive outpatient program (day treatment)

- Facilitated therapy group

- Individual therapy

- Psychiatric or medication consultation

- Informal support group for people in recovery

- Other: _____

Which of these activities do you currently do, and how often?

_____

_____

_____

_____

_____

Which would you like to start doing, and how often?

_____

_____

_____

_____

_____

For the next week, keep track of your recovery activities here: what you did and the result, if any.

Week of _____

| Day | Activity | Where | Time of day | With whom | For how long | Result |
|-----|----------|-------|-------------|-----------|--------------|--------|
| Sunday | | | | | | |
| Monday | | | | | | |
| Tuesday | | | | | | |
| Wednesday | | | | | | |
| Thursday | | | | | | |
| Friday | | | | | | |
| Saturday | | | | | | |

If you find it helpful to continue tracking your recovery-related activities, you can download a worksheet version of this exercise at http://www.newharbinger.com/52762.

# 15  Stretching Out of Your Comfort Zone

*PURPOSE:* To begin taking safe steps toward new and different life experiences by identifying your comfort zone and thinking about how you can move beyond it.

## DID YOU KNOW?

Sometimes the mere idea of creating a safe network and scheduling recovery-related activities might feel daunting. If you are someone who is shy, feels anxious in social situations, tends to isolate, or otherwise avoids people or unfamiliar situations, it can be especially challenging.

Changing habits is hard. For everyone. Remember the Stages of Change model from exercise 4? It's not like we, as creatures of habit, go marching forward from one stage to the next in a straight line. For most of us, it's three steps forward, one step back, or even cycling round and round, as we face our natural resistance to—and, often, fear of—change.

We all have a comfort zone—the things and objects, people, activities, environments, and habits that keep us feeling safe. But here's the catch. Changing habits in a big way, such as what you are doing in breaking free from your addiction to alcohol or drugs, inevitably involves some discomfort.

Have you seen this image before?

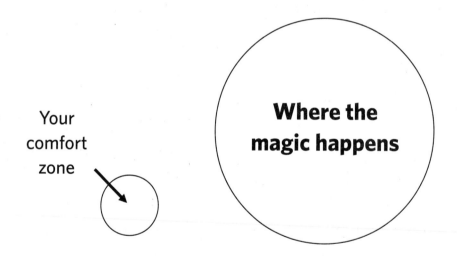

Isn't it great? First, notice that the MAGIC circle is a lot bigger than the COMFORT ZONE circle, which is encouraging. But see that empty space between the circles? That space represents the UNKNOWN, which can be both exciting and scary to most people, especially if you're giving up your go-to coping mechanism of using drugs or alcohol. How can you learn to safely cross that empty space?

Think about where you were before—actively using, likely unhappy with yourself, suffering from the pile of negative consequences that goes along with substance use. It was miserable, but at least it was familiar, right? Now that you're embracing sobriety, you'll have to navigate unknown territory.

Have you ever heard the saying "Leap, and the net will appear"? It's the same idea. This is where the "magic" comes into play—that is, moving toward something special, something different, maybe something unexpected, beyond what you've imagined or experienced so far in your life. Who knows what lies ahead? Yet what is the cost of staying still? As Yoda from the *Star Wars* movies said, "Do or do not. There is no try." And then you can ask yourself, "What's the worst that can happen?" Perhaps you'll stumble, but that's part of life too.

## DOES THIS SOUND LIKE YOU?

*Liliana, 22, lives at home with her parents, having dropped out of college because of failing grades and mild depression. She has been in and out of treatment for alcohol use since high school. She'll go a few months without drinking, and then she'll go on a bender. Then she'll stop again. She always feels bad about drinking but loves the sense of calm and relaxation alcohol gives her. She hasn't had a drink for a couple of months and feels more motivated than in the past to make some changes. Liliana attends a young people's AA meeting once a week and is thinking about asking for a temporary sponsor. Her parents are bugging her to "be productive," but she is not looking for a job or volunteer work. She sleeps late, watches TV, and texts with her old high school friends. She just started seeing a new therapist for her depression. "I just want to be happy for once in my life. But I don't know where to go or what to do, or how to break out of this same-old, same-old!"*

How are you like Liliana? How are you different?

_____

_____

_____

What clues in Liliana's story tell you that she might be stuck in her comfort zone? What could she do to get out?

_____

_____

_____

_____

# WHAT TO DO

In this exercise, you'll identify the components of your personal comfort zone. Next, you'll look back at the vision statement you wrote in exercise 2 to get some clues about "where the magic happens" for you—what will truly fulfill you, what you want your future to look like, where you feel a sense of hope and positive momentum. Then, you'll identify some concrete steps to take to guide you along your journey.

What are the components of your comfort zone? What helps you feel safe? Of course, feeling safe and protected is important to your recovery! This exercise is not about giving up everything comforting and familiar. It's about identifying the aspects of your comfort zone that might be interfering with your moving forward. Be as detailed as you can.

Things/Objects _____

_____

_____

People _____

_____

_____

Activities _____

_____

_____

Habits _____

_____

_____

Emotions _____

_____

_____

What are your thoughts and feelings about the unknown (that blank space between the circles)? What has helped in the past when you've succeeded in exploring the world outside of your comfort zone?

_____

_____

_____

_____

_____

_____

_____

_____

_____

_____

Next, look back at your vision statement in exercise 2. What items in that statement represent "where the magic happens" for you?

_____

_____

_____

_____

_____

_____

What steps are you willing to take to get closer to "where the magic happens" for you? Be detailed. Be optimistic while still being realistic.

Today _____

_____

_____

_____

Tomorrow _____

_____

_____

_____

In the next week _____

_____

_____

_____

In the next month _____

_____

_____

_____

In the next year _____

_____

_____

_____

# Know Your Feelings

# 16 Feelings 101—It's Okay to Be a Beginner

*PURPOSE:* To learn about your emotions by noticing and labeling different types of feelings.

## DID YOU KNOW?

In many cases, people in recovery from problem drug and alcohol use have been out of touch with their feelings, perhaps for a short time, perhaps a long time, perhaps forever. If you've been using for a long time, chances are that you've been numbing your emotions to some degree.

With sobriety, you are no longer numbing with substances, so you'll naturally feel more. Those feelings might include negative emotions such as fear, sadness, anger, shame, guilt, jealousy, or confusion; or positive emotions such as joy, calm, safety, gratitude, or pride.

If you grew up in a home where your genuine feelings were ignored or criticized or punished, you'll face challenges along the way, so be very kind and patient with yourself. Suddenly feeling your feelings can be exciting and motivating. But more often, at least at first, it can be overwhelming. In this exercise, you can begin to identify a range of feelings and work toward expressing them safely and effectively. By labeling our feelings, we can use the power of our mind to take a step back and assess, then make a good choice about what to do next.

## DOES THIS SOUND LIKE YOU?

*Olivia, 27, went to a rehab program and has not used any opiates for thirty days, after many years of use. She notices feeling "up and down" all the time but has difficulty identifying her feelings more specifically. "I was numb for so long. I kind of miss it, but I don't want to go back to using. How am I supposed to know what's normal or not normal? Is this anxiety or anger or just stress? Am I bored or depressed or sad?"*

How are you like Olivia? How are you different?

_____

_____

_____

Describe your own awareness of your feelings during this stage in your recovery.

_____

_____

_____

_____

## A Note on Boredom

Boredom is a common trigger to relapse. But boredom can often be a sign that you are disguising other feelings, such as sadness, depression, loneliness, anger, or even anxiety and fear. If you find yourself feeling bored, see if you can dig a little deeper to see what other feeling or feelings might lie beneath the boredom.

If you are used to being under the influence as a means of managing emotions, not being high or stoned or drunk will feel strange at first, and that can feel like boredom, too.

Write down your thoughts about boredom. What else might boredom be for you? What would it be like to be bored and not have to do anything about it—just witness it, sit with it, or let it pass without judgment?

_____

_____

_____

_____

_____

_____

_____

_____

_____

_____

## WHAT TO DO

In the chart that follows, you will record a few situations or experiences in which you are aware of your feelings. Start with just noticing the difference between *pleasant* and *unpleasant* feelings. Then, whenever you're ready, try to identify more specific words for what you might be feeling, and then reflect on what you noticed. A range of feelings is listed under each category. Feel free to write down any feelings that come to mind that might not appear on this list.

## PLEASANT

| | | | |
|---|---|---|---|
| affectionate | empowered | mellow | safe |
| amused | encouraged | open | satisfied |
| appreciative | excited | optimistic | secure |
| calm | friendly | passionate | strong |
| caring | fulfilled | peaceful | surprised |
| comfortable | grateful | pleased | thrilled |
| confident | hopeful | relaxed | trusting |
| curious | joyful | relieved | warm |
| delighted | loving | rested | |

## UNPLEASANT

| | | | |
|---|---|---|---|
| aggravated | disappointed | guarded | sad |
| agitated | disconnected | guilty | scared |
| ambivalent | discouraged | helpless | self-conscious |
| angry | disgusted | impatient | suspicious |
| annoyed | disheartened | insecure | tense |
| anxious | edgy | irritated | terrified |
| apprehensive | embarrassed | lonely | tired |
| ashamed | enraged | needy | uncomfortable |
| bad | exasperated | nervous | unhappy |
| bored | exhausted | overwhelmed | upset |
| confused | frightened | remorseful | vulnerable |
| contemptuous | frustrated | resentful | |
| depressed | furious | restless | |

| Day | Situation/experience when you noticed a feeling | Pleasant or unpleasant? | Specific feeling | Observations |
|---|---|---|---|---|
| Sunday | | | | |
| Monday | | | | |
| Tuesday | | | | |
| Wednesday | | | | |
| Thursday | | | | |
| Friday | | | | |
| Saturday | | | | |

If you find it helpful, you can download a worksheet version of this exercise to continue identifying your feelings at http://www.newharbinger.com/52762.

# 17  Responding, Not Reacting, to Feelings

*PURPOSE:* To manage difficult situations more skillfully by learning about the difference between reacting and responding.

## DID YOU KNOW?

Living a sober life means becoming familiar with and accepting of all your feelings and not turning to drugs or alcohol to escape or avoid them. Simply noticing your feelings, especially unpleasant ones, without necessarily acting on them can be a powerful skill for your sobriety.

The world is full of triggers that cause us to react and experience unpleasant feelings: uncooperative, unsympathetic, or demanding people; events and situations beyond our control; disappointments and dashed expectations; crazy drivers—the list goes on! Rather than ignoring our automatic reactions, we can learn to notice them and work with them.

## DOES THIS SOUND LIKE YOU?

As with any new skill, it takes practice and a willingness to experience something unfamiliar. Certain external events will always bother us, but if we learn to lower our reactivity and respond with wisdom and insight instead, we can make things better for ourselves, even if we can't change the world to our liking. Here is an example that shows how someone can learn to move from reacting to responding when faced with a difficult situation:

### Reacting

*Kenneth, 34, hasn't had a drink in thirty days. After a long, stressful day as a nurse, he arrives home tired, hoping for a peaceful evening with his family. Right away, his three-year-old son, upset about something, starts whining and clinging to him. He loves his son, but tonight, the last thing Kenneth wants to do is deal with a toddler. He feels his jaw clenching and his blood pressure surging and yells, "Stop it! Leave me alone!" His son wails louder, and then they're both miserable.*

Reacting happens in an instant, usually stemming from anger or fear or feeling overwhelmed. We all do it. Usually it happens when we're not thinking clearly or logically—it's a gut reaction.

### Responding

*Kenneth comes in the door after a long day and his toddler starts whining and clinging. Kenneth remembers hearing in his support group that when you're really stressed, it helps to stop, take a deep breath, and count to ten. After he does that, he notices that he feels tired and overwhelmed. He realizes his shoulders are tight, and he has a slight headache and jaw tension. His impulse is still to yell, but he stops himself because he is aware that yelling will only make the situation worse. Kenneth then stoops down and gives his son a big hug, and after a few moments, he asks his son what's wrong.*

When we respond, we can stop, notice what we're feeling and thinking, notice our body sensations, assess the situation, and then decide what to do next in a wiser, more thoughtful manner. That description is very similar to our definition of mindfulness—noticing what's happening in the present moment without judgment and with acceptance. Then, mindfully, we can choose what to do next.

Here, Kenneth turns his understandable stressed-out feelings into a positive action rather than popping off impulsively. He chooses a nonverbal response at first (hugging) because he can't initially trust that he won't say something he regrets. Then when they are both calm, he can approach his son with kind words.

How are you like Kenneth? How are you different?

_____

_____

_____

Can you think of times when you reacted—that is, became emotional without thinking through your response? What about a time or times when you responded wisely rather than reacted? Describe each instance below.

_____

_____

_____

_____

_____

_____

_____

# WHAT TO DO

Now that you are more familiar with your feelings, you can begin to notice where in your body you experience feelings and what their intensity is. This will help you respond instead of react. Remember not to judge yourself harshly if you do react. That won't help. Start with these steps:

**Step 1:** Take a deep breath. Better yet, take three conscious breaths (see exercise 1).

**Step 2:** Notice what you are feeling and where in your body you are feeling it (for example, jaw, neck, shoulders, chest, stomach).

**Step 3:** Note the intensity of the feeling (mild, moderate, strong).

**Step 4:** Let go of any tension you are aware of, to the best of your ability.

**Step 5:** Consider what is at stake—is it worth it to react with anger or impulsive actions? What will the consequence(s) be?

**Step 6:** Respond to the person or situation with compassion, using clear, simple language.

---

**Note:** If there's someone in your life who tends to trigger "reactions" instead of "responses" for you, you might plan to have an explicit conversation with them in which you acknowledge the dynamic. Explain that you're working to change your behavior as you try to moderate or end your substance use. Ask that person to support you in your efforts to change. Maybe you can even agree to practice this skill together!

---

This week, keep note of any incidents or experiences when you notice you reacted and shifted it into a response instead, and what the outcome was. Also write down the times when you found it hard to try responding and found yourself reacting instead, which is normal and understandable. Nobody is perfect. Ask yourself what was going on? What made it hard? What might you have done differently? With increased awareness of our feelings, we can make slow changes in our behavior over time. Step by step.

**Sunday**

Situation: _____

Reaction: _____

Feeling: _____ Intensity: _____

Where you felt it: _____

Response: _____

Outcome: _____

**Monday**

Situation: _____

Reaction: _____

Feeling: _____ Intensity: _____

Where you felt it: _____

Response: _____

Outcome: _____

**Tuesday**

Situation: _____

Reaction: _____

Feeling: _____ Intensity: _____

Where you felt it: _____

Response: _____

Outcome: _____

**Wednesday**

Situation: _____

Reaction: _____

Feeling: _____ Intensity: _____

Where you felt it: _____

Response: _____

Outcome: _____

**Thursday**

Situation: _____

Reaction: _____

Feeling: _____ Intensity: _____

Where you felt it: _____

Response: _____

Outcome: _____

**Friday**

Situation: _____

Reaction: _____

Feeling: _____ Intensity: _____

Where you felt it: _____

Response: _____

Outcome: _____

**Saturday**

Situation: _____

Reaction: _____

Feeling: _____ Intensity: _____

Where you felt it: _____

Response: _____

Outcome: _____

If you find it helpful, a downloadable worksheet for this exercise is available at http://www.newharbinger.com /52762.

# 18 Dear Substance of Choice

*PURPOSE:* To express some of your feelings about your substance of choice by writing a letter addressed directly to that substance.

## DID YOU KNOW?

If you've been drinking or using drugs for a while, maybe even a long while, saying good-bye to your familiar coping mechanism can be like saying good-bye to a dear friend. That's a normal, understandable part of the recovery process. It's also common, especially early on, to forget the bad times and to romanticize and glamorize the "good old days." Ultimately, you do have a relationship with that substance, for better or for worse.

Sometimes, people complain that their substance of choice has taken over their lives, as if that substance is a real being, a powerful entity that controls them—because that's exactly how it feels. Expressing your feelings in the form of a letter to your substance of choice can be an empowering act, like taking matters into your own hands.

## DOES THIS SOUND LIKE YOU?

*Jamar, 28, hasn't smoked marijuana in three weeks, after smoking several times a week since college. He quit because he has a great opportunity for a job as a salesman, and his interview is in another couple of weeks. His potential employer requires an initial drug test and then random drug testing. Jamar really wants this job, so he decides it's time to part ways with weed. At first, Jamar doesn't sleep well and has frequent headaches and some anxiety; those symptoms seem to be improving. But he really misses the feeling of getting high; he misses the excitement of buying a bag and all the activities involved in preparing to smoke. At night, he feels sad and lonely. He feels like something is missing from his life, something that gave him comfort and relief from the stresses of the day.*

How are you like Jamar? How are you different?

_____

_____

_____

Do you feel a sense of loss in parting ways with your substance of choice? Why or why not?

_____

_____

_____

_____

_____

_____

# WHAT TO DO

This exercise is designed to help you express those inevitable and normal feelings of loss. You'll also have the chance to recognize that there might be some mixed feelings and some downright positive feelings about saying good-bye to your substance of choice. The content of your letter will depend on where you are in the stages of change. If you're still using, this might be harder to write than if you have a few weeks or months of abstinence.

On the lines below, write a letter addressed directly to your substance of choice, like "Dear Vodka," "Dear Wine," "Dear Heroin," "Dear Cocaine," "Dear Weed," and so on. Use extra paper if needed. It might feel silly or weird at first, but remember, we do form relationships with the substances we use. And think about how much power that substance has had in your life. Now you get to talk to it and tell it what you really think and feel.

Write to the substance as if you are breaking up with a dear old friend or lover. You might tell your substance just how it has served you (in a positive way) over the years, how much you'll miss it, and how much you depended on it for certain things. You might also tell your substance how it has hurt you and interfered with your happiness and life goals. Tell your substance why you are choosing to move on from this relationship and how you feel about that decision.

Close your eyes for a moment and breathe. Now, dig down and be honest with yourself. Write your letter. Don't worry about grammar or punctuation or making it sound good. Just go for it!

Date _____

Dear _____,

_____

_____

_____

_____

_____

_____

_____

_____

_____

_____

_____

_____

_____

_____

_____

_____

_____

_____

_____

# Know Your Thoughts

# 19 Tracking Your Thoughts

*PURPOSE:* To strengthen your self-awareness by noticing your thoughts and keeping track of the habitual negative thoughts that might get in the way of your recovery.

## DID YOU KNOW?

Part of starting sober today involves the willingness to stop and listen to your thoughts, especially your negative thoughts, and what messages they are giving you about yourself, your feelings, and your behaviors. That's the essence of cognitive behavioral therapy—learning the connection among thoughts, feelings, and actions.

For most of us, with or without addictions, our thoughts often stream along their merry way without our even being conscious of them—they are automatic and habitual. Your boss criticizes you and, next thing you know, you're at the bar. Your friend doesn't return your phone call and, next thing you know, you pop a pill. You get a bad grade and, next thing you know, you light up a joint. You get the idea.

With practice and mindfulness, it is possible to drive an imaginary wedge between the initial thought and that seemingly automatic "next thing you know" moment. By learning to tune in to the "yakkety-yak" that inhabits our brains during most of our waking hours, you can not only identify those patterns of thought but, as you continue your sobriety, learn to identify your underlying feelings and make better, healthier choices about your actions. We'll talk in more depth about connecting thoughts and feelings in exercise 21. For now, let's just think about thinking.

## DOES THIS SOUND LIKE YOU?

*Jackson, 29, is a writer. Two of his short stories have been published in a prominent literary journal. He recently completed his first novel and has sent it out to a dozen agents. Jackson has had a drinking problem since college—bingeing on weekends, then trying, often unsuccessfully, to cut back during the week. He's experiencing more serious hangovers now than before. He recently heard about the Sober Curious movement, where folks often take a total timeout from drinking just to see what it's like. Jackson buddies up with another sober-curious friend for Dry January. Two weeks in, Jackson receives several rejections from agents. He automatically thinks, "My book sucks. I suck. I knew it. I'm just an imposter. No one will ever take me seriously. What is the point of continuing? I might as well get drunk." So he goes to the bar and has a drink. And then another.*

How are you like Jackson? How are you unlike him?

_____

_____

_____

Describe your typical reaction after experiencing a rejection or disappointment in your life.

_____

_____

_____

_____

# WHAT TO DO

In this exercise, you'll practice the mindful skill of noticing and recording what negative thoughts arise when something happens that makes you feel bad about yourself. These thoughts can come so quickly and automatically that we sometimes ignore them or, worse, misinterpret or distort them. Experts have identified various types of negative or distorted thoughts we can have; you can read more about those in exercise 20. But for now, just start noticing the dialogue in your head and record any habitual negative thoughts you become aware of over the next few weeks, then reflect briefly on the process.

| Date/Location | Situation | Thought | Reflection |
|---|---|---|---|
| Example: Monday at work. | Boss criticized me for turning in my report a day late. | Why does she always pick on me and no one else?<br><br>She has it in for me. Makes me want to pick up! | Wow. I think this way a lot, not just with my boss, but with other people too. |
|  |  |  |  |
|  |  |  |  |
|  |  |  |  |

| Date/Location | Situation | Thought | Reflection |
|---|---|---|---|
|  |  |  |  |
|  |  |  |  |
|  |  |  |  |
|  |  |  |  |
|  |  |  |  |

If you'd like to continue working with this tool, you'll find a worksheet at http://www.newharbinger.com/52762.

# 20 Labeling Your Thoughts

*PURPOSE:* To better manage your responses and reactions by identifying different types of cognitive distortions and applying them to your life situations.

## DID YOU KNOW?

The field of cognitive behavioral therapy (CBT) teaches about the connection between thoughts and actions. *Cognitive distortions* are types of thoughts that, if examined closely, turn out not to be true. These incorrect thoughts are often connected to certain core beliefs you hold about yourself. For example, deep down inside, you might believe that you are fundamentally bad, unlovable, defective, worthless, or a loser. Those core beliefs can affect your self-esteem, your relationships, and your ability to make healthy choices.

### Types of Cognitive Distortions

Now that you are becoming more mindful of what your thoughts are, let's take a closer look at a few types of cognitive distortions that people, with or without addictions, encounter. The more you are aware of your thinking processes, the more skilled you can become at preventing a relapse.

**Wearing a Filter:** Isolating and focusing on the negatives of a situation while ignoring or minimizing any positives. ("Nothing comes easily for me; so what if I graduated with a B average? I'm still just average.")

**Overgeneralizing:** Anticipating that a bad thing that happened once will happen again and again. ("Last time I visited my father, we got into a fight. I'm sure if I go there again, we'll just get into another fight.")

**Black-or-White Thinking:** Seeing things as either all good or all bad, with no gray area in between. ("No matter how hard I try, nothing good ever happens to me.")

**Jumping to Conclusions:** Making assumptions about people and events that might not be true. Two types of this cognitive distortion are mind reading ("My husband is thinking that I'm a lost cause") and fortune telling ("Even if I go to a treatment program, I'm sure I'll go back to using").

**Catastrophizing:** Expecting the worst to happen, no matter what. ("If I ask my boss for medical leave, he'll probably tell the whole staff, and then everyone will know and they'll judge me and avoid me, and I'll have to leave my job and then I'll be broke.")

**Personalizing:** Thinking everything that happens is related to us. ("Andrea was super irritable toward me today; she must not like me anymore.")

**Self-Blaming:** Thinking that everything bad that happens is your own fault, that you are inherently defective. ("Of course I didn't get that job. They could tell I'm not good enough. I'll never amount to anything.")

People in recovery from addictions often have specific thoughts related to their use that are also distorted but that feel true, out of habit. Can you relate to any of the categories below?

**Avoiding Pain:** Thinking that using drugs or alcohol will make it better. ("I'm so sad right now; one drink will help me beat the blues.")

**Looking for Pleasure:** Seeking the euphoria or elevated mood that drugs or alcohol can provide. ("I just want to have some fun! It will feel good!")

**Feeling Entitled:** Believing that you deserve to have what you want when you want it, despite the consequences. ("I worked hard this week. I deserve to get high.")

**Solving a Problem:** Turning to drugs or alcohol as a way to solve a problem that could be solved by other, less destructive, means. ("I'm so tired; I'll get a boost of energy if I snort this line.")

**Managing Stress:** When external circumstances are difficult to deal with, thinking substances will make a difference. ("I can't take all the bad news; just one pill won't hurt.")

## DOES THIS SOUND LIKE YOU?

*Daria, 28, is attending a day treatment program as a step-down from a monthlong residential program to treat her heroin addiction. She now has six weeks of abstinence and is taking prescribed Suboxone to help with cravings. This was her third attempt at rehab; in the past, she had refused medication and relapsed within two weeks of discharge. Her family insisted she attend the day program, but Daria is worried that this time will be like all the other times. "I'm just a hopeless addict. Nothing good ever happens to me, so why should I expect that this time is going to be the magic answer?"*

How are you like Daria? How are you unlike her?

_____

_____

_____

What cognitive distortions can you identify in Daria's thinking about this attempt at recovery?

_____

_____

_____

_____

_____

_____

## WHAT TO DO

Here, you'll build on the skills you began practicing in the previous exercise. Continue to notice and record your thoughts, especially the habitual negative thoughts you are aware of that are related to your recovery. This time, see if you can identify *which type* of cognitive distortion that thought might represent, and then reflect on the process.

| Date/Location | Situation | Thought | Type of thought | Reflection |
|---|---|---|---|---|
| Example from Daria, above: Sunday, NA meeting. | Listened to other people talk about their recovery. | I'm a hopeless addict. I'll never be like them. Everything I do ends up bad. | Black-or-white thinking, fortune telling, overgeneralizing. | I do this all the time—thinking I'm different or worse than others. Maybe I need to look at that pattern. |

| Date/Location | Situation | Thought | Type of thought | Reflection |
|---|---|---|---|---|
|  |  |  |  |  |
|  |  |  |  |  |
|  |  |  |  |  |
|  |  |  |  |  |
|  |  |  |  |  |

If you'd like to continue working with this tool, you'll find a worksheet at http://www.newharbinger.com/52762.

# 2I Connecting Your Thoughts and Feelings

*PURPOSE:* To improve your awareness of how your negative thoughts might influence your feelings by tracking their connection.

## DID YOU KNOW?

If you have been practicing noticing and labeling your thoughts, especially your negative thoughts, you're undoubtedly aware that certain lines of thought can generate certain difficult feelings. Habitual negative thoughts can make us feel lonely, worthless, ashamed, guilty, sad, angry, frustrated, irritated, anxious, or scared—sometimes mildly, sometimes intensely.

One key to breaking free from addiction is to get better and better at linking up your thoughts with your feelings. You are learning to be mindful of that connection; that is, you are learning to stop, notice what you're thinking, and reflect on your thoughts. Congratulations! Now we'll look at the next step: connecting your thoughts and feelings.

## DOES THIS SOUND LIKE YOU?

*Kwame, 34, is a software engineer who works over sixty hours a week at a fast-paced tech company. He has a history of binge drinking on weekends and multiple attempts at total abstinence. Sometimes, he can go for a few weeks without a drink, but he has noticed that whenever he does slip, it's on a Friday, after work. "I can't help it. I just want that reward at the end of a hard week, so I stop at my favorite liquor store on the way home." With the help of a counselor, Kwame decided to try noticing the pattern of his thoughts as follows:*

*Situation* → *Habitual thought* → *Type of thought* → *Reflection*

See exercise 20 to identify some different types of thoughts.

| Situation | Habitual thought | Type of thought | Reflection |
|---|---|---|---|
| Example: Passed liquor store on way home, had urge, bought two nips, got buzzed. | I deserve a break. It's been a hard week. It'll feel so good. <br><br> Afterward: I wish I hadn't given in to temptation again. I'm such a loser. | Feeling entitled, looking for pleasure, self-blaming. | This happens a lot. <br><br> Maybe I need to ask for help in sorting out the pattern. |

How are you like Kwame? How are you different?

_____

_____

_____

What do you think Kwame is actually feeling? Name one or two emotions. Refer to the feelings list in exercise 16 for some options, if needed.

_____

_____

_____

_____

_____

## WHAT TO DO

In this exercise, you'll add the *feeling or feelings* to the chain you've been working on. For the next week, record any situation when you are triggered to use drugs or alcohol, whether or not you actually do. The chain of events often happens quickly and subconsciously. Noticing and recording the connections is an act of personal empowerment. You are saying, "I am not just a victim of circumstances out of my control. I can get to know myself and learn to take charge of the behaviors that stem from my thoughts and feelings." On the following page is an example of Kwame's recording of thoughts, with the addition of labeling his feelings.

| Date/Location | Situation | Habitual thought | Type of thought | Feeling | Reflection |
|---|---|---|---|---|---|
| Example: Friday after work. | Passed liquor store on way home, had urge, bought two nips, got buzzed. | I deserve a break. It's been a hard week. It'll feel so good. | Feeling entitled, looking for pleasure, self-blaming. | Angry, frustrated, stressed out, resentful, sad. | I'm so stressed out by Friday. I can see why I turn to alcohol for a reward, but then I feel ashamed and guilty. Next time, I'll call a friend for support and find something else pleasurable to do to reward myself. |
|  |  |  |  |  |  |
|  |  |  |  |  |  |
|  |  |  |  |  |  |
|  |  |  |  |  |  |

# 22 Mindful Self-Compassion

*PURPOSE:* To improve your sense of well-being by learning two self-compassionate practices.

## DID YOU KNOW?

You deserve compassion. You are a human being, wonderful and flawed, like all human beings. And, like many people in recovery from substance use, you probably have a long history of being down on yourself. In addition, you might have experienced a great deal of suffering in your life, without anyone to offer compassion or comfort, and that could be a reason you have sought comfort in substances. The world might not always offer you all the love and support you need, but what about offering yourself compassion?

Self-compassion is not the same as self-pity. It is not being selfish. It is a healthy, effective way to heal yourself and move forward in your recovery. Much research exists to show the psychological benefits of mindful self-compassion, a practice derived from the Buddhist concept of lovingkindness and developed formally in the West by psychologists Kristin Neff and Christopher Germer, among others (Neff 2023; Neff and Germer 2013).

Neff (2003) identified three key components of mindful self-compassion: mindfulness (vs. overidentification), self-kindness (vs. self-criticism), and common humanity (vs. isolation). We've discussed *mindfulness* earlier (see exercise 1). Here, the reference to "overidentification" refers to our tendency to get tangled up in our thoughts and feelings and lose perspective. The notion of *self-kindness* is more of an attitude than a technique—adopting a loving, caring relationship toward yourself and treating yourself kindly, the way you might treat a close friend or loved one or a beloved pet. *Common humanity* is the idea that *you are not alone.*

Pause for a moment and really take that in. You are not alone in your suffering; many people are experiencing or have experienced similar struggles. This piece of mindful self-compassion in no way minimizes your individual pain and challenges. Instead, it can help you feel less isolated, less "defective" or "different," and remind you that support and understanding are indeed available out there in the world.

## DOES THIS SOUND LIKE YOU?

*Anthony, 35, has been sober from drugs and alcohol for a year. He is married, works full time in construction, and visits his parents every weekend to help them around the house. Anthony has always had high expectations of himself to be perfect and please others. He criticizes himself when he doesn't live up to those internal expectations. When Anthony tunes in to his thoughts, much of what he hears is criticism, which makes him miserable. He suspects that's part of what drove him to use in the first place. Now that he's sober, Anthony is trying to tell that harsh "inner critic" to "just shut up and leave me alone," but that strategy is not working. In fact, the self-criticism is getting a little worse.*

How are you like Anthony? How are you unlike him?

_____

_____

_____

What types of compassionate statements would you want to say to Anthony to help him lower the volume on the self-criticism?

_____

_____

_____

_____

# WHAT TO DO

In this exercise, you will have an opportunity to practice two ways of offering yourself compassion: kind words and kind touch. These practices can be a powerful way to reconnect—or connect for the very first time—with the parts of yourself that need, want, and deserve to be seen, loved, and appreciated. Sometimes, deep feelings of grief and longing can arise when we offer ourselves simple acts of compassion. That is a normal and natural outcome at first. So take it slow. And take it in as best you can.

## Kind Words

To get started, think of some things that you might say to a friend or family member whom you care about a lot who might be going through a hard time and needs your support. Write these phrases below.

_____

_____

_____

_____

_____

Now, think of a situation when you were down on yourself and wishing someone were there to help you out. What was the situation? What were you feeling at the time?

_____

_____

_____

_____

_____

What are some kind and compassionate phrases you could say to yourself on a regular basis, even when you're not facing a challenging situation, as above? If you have trouble thinking of something to say to yourself, look at the phrases you wrote that you might say to a loved one who is hurting, and write them here, perhaps using the first person "I." You may also find some helpful phrases in the following list:

| | |
|---|---|
| I am okay as I am. | I forgive myself. |
| I am a good person. | I have normal needs and desires. |
| I love myself. | I am allowed to make mistakes. |
| I am trying hard and deserve support. | I am imperfect and it's okay to be imperfect. |
| I have a lot to offer. | I am a kind, loving person. |
| | |

Now select two or three specific phrases that you would like to repeat to yourself as you begin your self-compassion practice and list them here.

_____

_____

_____

_____

_____

## Kind Touch

Another way to express mindful self-compassion is through giving yourself a kind touch or gesture. In the same way that someone might physically comfort you when you're hurting, you can do that for yourself. You might stroke your hand or arm or cheek gently; place your hand over your heart area and hold it there gently; or give yourself a big, delicious bear hug. We all need safe, loving touch—it's a gift you can offer yourself at any time of the day or night. You deserve it.

You may want to start by practicing self-compassion in response to some negative feeling that gets triggered. You may also include mindful self-compassion as part of your regular sobriety activities. Just like exercise or meditation, the more you practice, the more you reap the benefits!

Set aside time each day, maybe when you wake up or as you're falling asleep, to try your chosen phrases and/or gestures, even when you're feeling good about yourself. Do it as many times as you like and record your experience with kind words and kind touch in the chart below.

| Date/Time | Situation? What were you feeling? | Self-compassionate phrase and/or gesture? | Response/Reflection |
|---|---|---|---|
| | | | |
| | | | |
| | | | |
| | | | |
| | | | |
| | | | |
| | | | |

If you'd like to continue working with this tool, you'll find a worksheet at http://www.newharbinger.com/52762.

# 23  Revising Your Inner Dialogue

*PURPOSE:* To minimize the likelihood of adverse consequences by learning how to reframe negative thoughts into more positive, self-compassionate ones.

## DID YOU KNOW?

You might have noticed how quickly your negative thoughts can result in harmful, impulsive actions, often without you either noticing or honoring your feelings. The more you're aware of your thoughts and feelings, however, the more you can change direction toward a more positive outcome even when you're faced with strong feelings or triggering thoughts.

Revising your inner dialogue is not the same as positive thinking. You might have heard about the *Saturday Night Live* character Stuart Smalley, who hosted a satirical self-help show called *Daily Affirmation with Stuart Smalley*. After offering advice to others, Stuart would stand in front of a full-length mirror and repeat the following words: "You're good enough, you're smart enough, and doggone it, people like you."

There's nothing wrong with positive self-talk. But if you are working on starting a sober life today, you'll need to learn how to work actively with the negative thoughts you have—exploring where they come from and how to transform them. You've already got some great beginning skills when it comes to responding more wisely, restructuring negative thoughts, and practicing self-compassion. Now let's see how you can fit all of these ideas together to develop a new, healthier, happier inner dialogue.

## DOES THIS SOUND LIKE YOU?

Let's go back to Kwame, the software engineer from exercise 21 with a history of weekend binge drinking.

> *Kwame was able to notice his pattern of rewarding himself with alcohol on Friday nights, and when he considered the emotions that drove this pattern, he said he was "angry," "frustrated," "stressed out," "resentful," and "sad." When he considered his behavior, he reflected that the alcohol didn't actually help him. But Kwame is so used to being down on himself, he thinks he's doomed to repeat the same pattern.*

How are you like Kwame? How are you different?

_____

_____

_____

How do you think Kwame's negative thinking is affecting his drinking?

_____

_____

_____

# WHAT TO DO

Begin by writing down an example of a typical inner dialogue—that is, the narrative that you (and most of us) have going on in our heads about our behavior, choices, values, worth, and so on.

For example, here is a peek at Kwame's typical inner dialogue:

*I work so hard, I deserve a reward at the end of the week. I mean, what's the harm in having one drink? It tastes great and makes me relax. But then I feel ashamed and guilty. I'm hopeless. This whole cycle makes me feel helpless and out of control. I don't know how to get out of this pattern. Maybe I'm just doomed to be an alcoholic for the rest of my life. Would that be so horrible?*

You can see that Kwame has different sides to his feelings—here, we see the part that feels he deserves the reward of a drink and the part that is ashamed and upset about his choice to drink. Sound familiar? If so, you're not alone.

Record your typical inner dialogue below. You might refer to the situations, thoughts, and feelings that you have been noticing and tracking in the previous exercises, or you might refer to a new situation that you've become aware of. Write down the way the dialogue typically plays out, without censoring or editing or worrying about grammar, punctuation, or spelling.

_____

_____

_____

_____

_____

_____

_____

Next, try revising that dialogue. Before you start writing, you might want to reflect on the following questions:

- What could I say to myself instead?

- How could I reframe this thought or feeling into something more positive and self-compassionate?

- What action could I take to try to change these painful patterns?

As an example, take a look at Kwame's revised inner dialogue:

*Ouch. I can see how I'm beating myself up all the time with the back and forth. It hurts. I'm not a bad person. I do work hard, and I'm at the top of my game. And I'm proud of that. But drinking isn't solving anything. It's making things worse. I care about my health. Making change is scary. I think the bottom line is that my long hours are taking a toll. I'm exhausted and drained. I need a break! On Monday, I will ask to meet with my boss to discuss cutting back on my hours. And maybe instead of stopping at the liquor store on Fridays, I can plan an evening out with friends. It's been a while since I've hung out with my buddies because I'm always so beat. They'll understand about my not drinking—in fact, my friend Cal is in AA. Maybe I'll go to a meeting with him. I want to feel better about myself.*

Now write down your answers to the questions noted above and expand your dialogue as needed.

_____

_____

_____

_____

_____

_____

_____

Great job! You may keep revising and refining this inner dialogue as you continue on your path to sobriety. You may also want to try this exercise with other typical inner dialogues you become aware of. And, just like the best writers, you can even revise your revisions as many times as you want!

If you'd like to continue working with this tool, you'll find a worksheet at http://www.newharbinger.com/52762.

# The
# Mind-Body
# Connection

# 24  First, Unplug!

> *PURPOSE:* To learn how to relax your mind and body by identifying and limiting the activities in your life that cause stress and keep your mind on "alert."

## DID YOU KNOW?

Most of us live in a world full of stimulation—TV, radio, music, smartphones, computers, video games, traffic, road construction, and other environmental noises. Sometimes it's out of our control—for instance, if you're a parent, kids can be on full tilt full time. Sometimes, we seek out the stimulation, perhaps to avoid feelings, perhaps because silence feels scary or uncomfortable.

Studies show that constant stimulation and mental activity can lead to depression, anxiety, attention and memory problems, and difficulty concentrating or focusing, all of which can be big challenges to staying on your path to sobriety.

Give your brain a break. That doesn't mean you need to go to a silent meditation retreat, although that might be a goal someday. You can experiment with simple ways to take breaks from all the noise and stimulation.

## DOES THIS SOUND LIKE YOU?

*From the moment Tamika, 26, wakes up in the morning, she is wired to technology—checking her phone in bed, listening to the car radio, wearing earbuds at her job, watching TV at night, and texting with friends and family any chance she gets. She now has six weeks of abstinence from cocaine and says she misses the feeling of being "up." But she doesn't miss the crash that used to follow, which is why she decided to quit. Newly sober, Tamika is sleeping even less and using social media even more than before. Sometimes she thinks about smoking marijuana to help her relax.*

How are you like Tamika? How are you different?

_____

_____

_____

What would you suggest to Tamika to help her relax her mind without using substances?

_____

_____

_____

_____

_____

## WHAT TO DO

Here is a list of things that might be keeping you from relaxing your mind. Which ones are particular issues for you? Check them off, and then add any others to the list in the spaces provided.

- ☐ Checking email
- ☐ Checking Facebook, Instagram, TikTok, etc.
- ☐ Dealing with childcare responsibilities
- ☐ Dealing with job demands
- ☐ Driving with the radio on
- ☐ Going from meeting to meeting
- ☐ Going out to clubs
- ☐ Going to loud outdoor concerts
- ☐ Going to parties
- ☐ Listening to music with earbuds

- ☐ Posting or reading posts on social media
- ☐ Talking on the phone
- ☐ Texting
- ☐ Viewing other social media
- ☐ Visiting friends and family
- ☐ Watching TV
- ☐ Other: _____
- ☐ Other: _____
- ☐ Other: _____
- ☐ Other: _____

What are the top three items from the list above that are getting in the way of relaxing your mind?

1. _____

2. _____

3. _____

Do you have a choice about that activity (for example, childcare vs. TikTok)? If not, can you ask for help in getting a break? Describe your current situation.

_____

_____

_____

If you want to cut back, when and how much will you allow yourself to do this activity—for example, check TikTok (or other social media sites) only three times a day for no more than five minutes or turn off the TV after 9:00 p.m.? Be very specific. It might help to find an "unplugging" buddy—someone who's trying to cut back too, so you can share your progress together at the end of each day.

Name of person/buddy: _____

How do you feel about cutting back on or eliminating the activities that interfere with relaxing your mind?

_____

_____

_____

Here, it's crucial to remember the skills you've begun to build in previous exercises, including "Connecting Your Thoughts and Feelings" (exercise 21) and "Mindful Self-Compassion" (exercise 22). If you're feeling ambivalence or reluctance about changing, that's totally normal. You also have the capacity to acknowledge those tough feelings and work with them, even as you consciously choose what you will actually do to support a sober, healthy life.

Also remember the safe network you created in exercise 12. Can you ask some of the people on that list for help getting going or staying on track, when you feel you need support?

Use this chart to keep track of your "unplugging" activities. (If you'd like a worksheet version of this activity, visit http://www.newharbinger.com/52762.)

| Day | Activity you unplugged from | For how long? | How did you feel before? During? After? If you have an "unplugging buddy," did you report to them? How was that? |
|-----|------------------------------|----------------|---------------------------------------------------------------------------------------------------------------------|
|     |                              |                |                                                                                                                     |
|     |                              |                |                                                                                                                     |
|     |                              |                |                                                                                                                     |
|     |                              |                |                                                                                                                     |
|     |                              |                |                                                                                                                     |
|     |                              |                |                                                                                                                     |

# 25  Mindful Breathing

*PURPOSE:* To enhance your mind-body connection by learning and practicing several mindful breathing exercises.

## DID YOU KNOW?

It's often hard—both in early recovery and in ongoing recovery—for people breaking free from substance addiction to experience being in their bodies without being under the influence. Many people with addiction histories are aware that they are consciously choosing to be numb, check out, relieve anxiety, treat depression, experience a buzz, expand their consciousness, avoid emotional pain, treat physical pain, and so on. And many people with addiction histories do so for good reason—they might have experienced trauma, and "checking out" has long served as a protective and effective coping mechanism.

As you embark on a sober life, you are learning how to be in your body and becoming aware of the range of sensations that arise. Some might be pleasant, some unpleasant. Can you imagine just sitting with whatever sensations arise, watching them come and go, without being triggered to use? If the answer is no, that's okay. It's never too late to learn.

As challenging as it might be, learning to pay attention to your breathing is a wonderful beginning mindfulness skill that can go a long way to prevent you from reacting to stress or triggers by automatically picking up. You already learned about taking three conscious breaths at the beginning of this book (exercise 1). Now you'll learn several exercises designed to bring awareness to your breath and your mind-body connection.

Learning to be in your body comfortably can take time. Be patient. As noted in exercise 1, if focusing on the breath causes anxiety or distress, it's fine to hold off for now and do a different exercise, such as "5-4-3-2-1 Grounding" (exercise 1).

## DOES THIS SOUND LIKE YOU?

*Carter, 19, was diagnosed with ADD (attention deficit disorder) when he was eight and put on a variety of stimulants, such as Ritalin and Adderall. Eventually, he developed a serious Adderall use disorder and started buying it from friends and then dealing it on campus as a college freshman. He was suspended for one semester and then couldn't get a doctor to prescribe him stimulants anymore. Now, in his mandatory counseling, he is required to attend mindfulness and meditation classes, but he is resistant. Carter says he can't possibly sit still and "be with" his racing mind and jumpy body, as the instructor suggests.*

How are you like Carter? How are you different?

_____

_____

_____

What are your thoughts and feelings, both positive and negative, about the suggestion to practice tuning in to your breath?

_____

_____

_____

_____

_____

_____

## WHAT TO DO

Here are three simple breathing exercises that you can try this week. Choose the ones that might be a good fit for you. Sit in a comfortable position in a chair or on a meditation cushion. Avoid slouching. In each case, if your mind starts generating a lot of thoughts, which it inevitably will, gently bring your attention back to your breath.

**In-and-Out Breathing:** Set a timer for two minutes (at first, then gradually work up to four or five minutes per sitting). Quiet your mind as best as you can and simply notice your breath going in and out. Don't push or strain or try to control your breathing in any way. Notice: Does the air enter through your nose? Your mouth? Just notice. Inhale. Exhale. Slow. Easy. No effort. Notice your chest or your belly rising and falling as you discover the rhythm and pace of your breathing.

**Counting Breaths:** Sit comfortably and eliminate any distractions. Inhale slowly, counting up to five. One, two, three, four, five. Exhale slowly, counting down from five. Five, four, three, two, one. You may wish to hold the breath for one or two counts before exhaling. Whatever counting pattern you choose, be sure not to strain or force your breathing. Easy, steady, in and out.

**Belly Breathing:** Sit comfortably or lie down on a mat or soft carpet (avoid the bed, as you might fall asleep). Put one hand on your belly and the other hand on your chest. Close your mouth and breathe in through your nose, deeply inhaling but not straining. Notice your belly rising but keep your chest still. Exhale the air through your mouth, noticing your belly contracting slightly. Repeat up to ten times.

Keep track of your progress on the chart below, noting which exercise you did, when, and for how long you practiced each day. Note how it made you feel.

If you'd like a downloadable copy of this tracking form, visit http://www.newharbinger.com/52762. For other breathing exercises, you may do a search on YouTube for "mindful breathing," or search the web for other resources; there are many.

| Day | Type of breathing | When and where you practiced | For how long? | How did it feel? |
|---|---|---|---|---|
| Sunday | | | | |
| Monday | | | | |
| Tuesday | | | | |
| Wednesday | | | | |
| Thursday | | | | |
| Friday | | | | |
| Saturday | | | | |

# 26 Body Scan

*PURPOSE:* To experience physical and mental relaxation by learning and practicing the body scan technique.

## DID YOU KNOW?

Again, practicing and building tolerance for being present in your body is one key to recovering from problem substance use—and avoiding relapse. The ability to be present in your body can help you interrupt the automatic cycle by which thoughts lead to urges, which can then lead to impulsive actions or reactions. Sometimes an urge is experienced physically, before any awareness of the thought—and the more awareness you can bring to this process, the more sense of empowerment and control you can build over your choices.

In this exercise, you'll learn another way to relax the body and mind as you begin to notice your experience *just as it is*. It's called the body scan, which is exactly as it sounds. While sitting or lying in a comfortable position, you'll bring your mind's awareness to one part of your body at a time, scanning up from the feet to the head. In the body scan, you can learn to notice your physical sensations without needing to do anything about them. This takes practice and patience. Approaching this exercise with a spirit of curiosity can help. Rather than "Uh-oh! My heart is beating fast," for example, you can practice saying, "Oh. I feel my heart beating. Well, let me just feel it beat and notice what that's like. Nothing bad is happening. I can be with my body as it is."

## DOES THIS SOUND LIKE YOU?

*Robert, 31, a landscaper, is recovering from heroin addiction and occasional illicit fentanyl use. He went through a medically supervised discontinuation program and is now taking prescribed buprenorphine, a medicine for opiate dependence. He no longer has physical withdrawal symptoms, is seeing a therapist he likes, and is feeling stable and proud of himself. His long-term goal is to stay sober without medication; Robert and his doctor are planning to assess the possibility of tapering safely down from his medication after at least six months of stabilization. As his body and mind are adjusting, Robert worries that, if and when he stops the medication, he will be tempted to relapse. He wants to learn some mindfulness and relaxation skills now in support of his wish to "be here now."*

How are you like Robert? How are you different?

_____

_____

_____

What has been your experience, if any, with body-focused relaxation exercises? Describe.

_____

_____

_____

_____

_____

How important is the mind-body connection to you in your own recovery process? How do you feel about learning mindfulness skills as a relapse prevention strategy? Describe.

_____

_____

_____

_____

_____

# WHAT TO DO

Now you'll try the body scan. Set aside twenty to thirty minutes for this exercise. Or, if that feels like too much at first, try ten to start. But don't rush through it—give yourself the gift of this experience of being in your one and only body.

If, as you practice, you find your thoughts drifting off, simply bring your mind back to focusing on that part of your body. You may keep your eyes open or closed; it's up to you. If you prefer to listen to the body scan, you can access the audio version at http://www.newharbinger.com/52762. (Many other body scan audio or video recordings exist online, including some lovely ones on YouTube.)

Begin by simply noticing your body. Notice any sensations you might be feeling—aches, itches, tingles; notice any feelings you might be aware of—calm, serenity, fear, anxiety. Whatever it is for you, just notice without judgment and with acceptance. There's nothing you need to do. Nothing bad is happening in this moment.

Feel the weight of your body. Notice your body on the chair or the floor.

Take several long, deep breaths. Notice your chest or belly expanding, bringing air into your lungs, helping you relax.

Starting with your feet, notice any sensations—tension, vibrations, temperature, or pressure. There is no right or wrong. Just notice. If you notice that you are holding some tension at any point during this body scan, release that tension as best as you can.

Progress up through your body, from the feet to the ankles, calves, knees, thighs, hips, buttocks, pelvis, abdomen, chest, hands, arms, shoulders, back, neck, jaw, face, and scalp. Each time, notice any tension, vibrations, temperature, or pressure.

Continue to breathe deeply and slowly. Come back to noticing your entire body, connecting all parts together, just noticing without judgment and with acceptance.

Take a few deep breaths and come back into the present moment slowly and with kindness.

When you do the body scan, record what it was like either here or on the form available at http://www.harbinger.com/52762. An audio recording with relaxing music is also available at this link

| When and where you practiced | For how long? | How did it feel? |
| --- | --- | --- |
| | | |
| | | |
| | | |
| | | |
| | | |
| | | |
| | | |

# 27 Progressive Muscle Relaxation

*PURPOSE:* To enhance your mind-body connection by learning and practicing a progressive muscle relaxation exercise.

## DID YOU KNOW?

Progressive muscle relaxation is another tool to help you be more aware of your body and release stress and tension. With mindful breathing or the body scan, you are not actively moving any parts of your body—you are simply noticing and watching your thoughts and feelings without judgment and with acceptance.

This time, you'll be scanning through your body, as before, but you'll be tensing and releasing individual muscle groups as you go. By doing so, you not only get the physical benefit of relaxing your muscles, but you also increase your awareness of your body, which is an important element of the mind-body connection that can help you stay sober.

Tensing and releasing your muscles is great for stress reduction. You consciously create the stress (tension) and then take charge of letting it go (release). Tense. Release. *Ahh!*

Becoming more aware of what is happening in your body can help you break free from your addiction, bringing a sense of empowerment rather than victimization. "I can notice and make choices about what's happening in my body, even if it isn't always pleasant" is a very different statement from "I can't stand feeling these sensations; I'm helpless to control what's happening to me."

## DOES THIS SOUND LIKE YOU?

*Sophia, 37, has been sober from alcohol and drugs for four years. She lives alone and works as a case manager at a treatment center for women survivors of domestic violence. Sophia finds her job rewarding but stressful, as there are frequent crises and days filled with high emotions. Now, instead of using after work, Sophia overeats to feel numb. "I know I'm substituting one substance for another, but I don't know how else to manage my stress," she says. She has developed frequent migraines and complains of lower-back pain.*

How are you like Sophia? How are you different?

_____

_____

_____

Do you sometimes use another substance as a substitute for your substance of choice to manage your stress? Describe it.

_____

_____

_____

_____

Do you experience any physical signs and symptoms of stress, such as migraines? What are you doing to manage them?

_____

_____

_____

_____

# WHAT TO DO

Now, you'll try progressive muscle relaxation. Set aside about twenty minutes if you plan to do the full exercise described below. You can also do a shorter version with just the upper body or just the lower body. An audio version of this exercise is available at http://www.newharbinger.com/52762.

Begin by lying down or sitting comfortably in a chair. Start with your feet, noticing any tension. Create more tension by tightening the muscles in your feet and ankles, scrunching your toes. Squeeze hard, as hard as you can, and hold for about five to ten seconds, then release. Notice the change in your experience from the tensed muscles to the relaxed ones. Feel the difference.

Progress slowly up through your body, from the feet to the ankles, calves, thighs, hips, buttocks, pelvis, abdomen, chest, hands, lower arms, upper arms, shoulders, back, neck, jaw, and face. Each time, tense, hold, and release.

Be sure to breathe as slowly and steadily as you can, noticing the difference between tension and relaxation.

When you are ready, slowly come back to the present moment. Wake up your feet and hands, shaking them out if you wish. Before you resume regular activity, take a few moments just to rest and breathe.

Record when you do the progressive muscle relaxation exercise and what it was like. You can do that here or on the form available at http://www.newharbinger.com/52762. An audio recording with relaxing music is also available at this link

| When and where you practiced | For how long? | How did it feel? |
|---|---|---|
|  |  |  |
|  |  |  |
|  |  |  |
|  |  |  |
|  |  |  |
|  |  |  |
|  |  |  |

# 28 Taking a "Noticing" Walk

*PURPOSE:* To bring awareness to the present moment by taking a walk outside and noticing your environment using all your senses.

## DID YOU KNOW?

One key component of mindfulness is being aware not just of what's going on inside you (thoughts, feelings, sensations) but also what's going on outside of your body and mind. While the breathing, body scan, and progressive muscle relaxation exercises are aimed at increasing your internal awareness in a nonjudgmental, accepting manner, taking a mindful walk is a bit different.

These days, more and more people are walking around outdoors while looking down at their phones, whether it's at the beach, the lake, the mountains, or just around the neighborhood. We're wired up all the time. Studies even show that looking at our phones constantly is changing our brains to be more active (Greenfield 2015) as we seek the next exciting stimulus and scroll from thing to thing to thing, never really stopping to notice (see also exercise 24).

Learning to be present in the moment and lowering your reactivity will help with relapse prevention. Mindful walking in a beautiful environment is ideal for waking up the senses and noticing what's around us. We don't always have access to a beautiful environment, though, so taking a mindful walk in a busy city environment can be a good exercise as well. Ultimately, the idea is to give yourself the experience of shifting your perspective outward while remaining connected to your body, your thoughts, and your feelings.

## DOES THIS SOUND LIKE YOU?

*Thomas, 29, is a newly divorced IT manager who works about fifty hours a week. Last year, he was hospitalized for using a combination of alcohol and Klonopin, an antianxiety medication that he was using without a prescription. Thomas has been seeing a therapist for nearly ten years to work on recovering from the trauma of childhood physical and sexual abuse. He has stopped using Klonopin but still drinks occasionally to, as he says, "steady his nerves." His therapist has recommended meditation and yoga and other mind-body relaxation techniques, but Thomas finds that his anxiety spikes during some of these exercises, which triggers him to want to use. "I hate sitting still and noticing what's happening in my body," he says. "It just makes things worse."*

How are you like Thomas? How are you different?

_____

_____

_____

Have you ever experienced anxiety at being told "You really should meditate or do deep breathing to relax"? What did you do or not do in response?

_____

_____

_____

_____

Are you open to trying a different way to be mindful? Why or why not?

_____

_____

_____

_____

# WHAT TO DO

Go for a walk outside by yourself for a minimum of fifteen to twenty minutes. (In cold weather, you might choose a museum or library.) Turn off your phone—or leave it at home if you possibly can! Notice any sounds, really tuning in to everything you can hear—sounds up close, sounds at a medium distance, sounds far away. Take it all in. Notice what you feel in your body when you do this, without judgment and with acceptance.

As an alternative to a "listening" walk, you might choose to notice the smells in your environment. How many different smells can you notice? What smells pleasant (for example, a flower)? What smells unpleasant (for example, car exhaust, the scent of a skunk)? Notice what you feel in your body when you do this.

Noticing what you see is another type of mindful walk. Notice colors, shapes, sizes, and contrasts. Look up to the sky. Look down to the ground. Take it all in, consciously. Notice what you feel in your body when you do this.

If you experience some anxiety at being outdoors and opening up your senses, reassure yourself that nothing bad is happening. You could do a simple, similar exercise that will help focus your mind and calm your body, such as "Grounding 5-4-3-2-1" (exercise 1), or identify everything in your environment that is red, or green, or another color. You can also tell yourself everything will be okay, or repeat your self-compassionate statements (exercise 22) as you walk. Congratulate yourself for trying. Be creative and do what feels good for you.

When you get home, record the sounds, smells, and sights in as much detail as you can remember, and what it was like for you. (If you find this practice and tracking it helpful, you'll find a worksheet for this exercise at http://www.newharbinger.com/52762.)

| When and where you practiced | For how long? | What did you notice? | How did it feel? |
|---|---|---|---|
| | | | |
| | | | |
| | | | |
| | | | |
| | | | |
| | | | |
| | | | |

# 29  Eating a Mindful Meal

*PURPOSE:* To boost your enjoyment of food by learning to eat mindfully.

## DID YOU KNOW?

When is the last time you noticed, really noticed, what you were eating and what you were doing while eating? So much stress, so many responsibilities—it's easy to end up mindlessly inhaling your food while you sneak one more peek at your phone or simply rush toward the day's finish line.

Sobriety means more than just stopping your problem substance use. It means learning to enjoy what life has to offer. And, as we will explore more in exercise 31, eating good, enjoyable food is one of life's greatest pleasures. Bringing mindful awareness to your food through expanding your sensory awareness can enrich your whole day and help you stay in the present moment.

## DOES THIS SOUND LIKE YOU?

*Clarissa, 38, is a married mother of two who is in recovery from problem alcohol use. After staying home with the kids until they were old enough to go to school, Clarissa now works part time as an office manager; her husband is an Uber driver who works evenings, so she usually prepares a simple meal or, more often, picks up some fast food on her way home. Clarissa says she doesn't pay much attention to her food—"It's never been a big priority. I could be eating flavored cardboard for all I know. I just don't notice what goes in my mouth."*

How are you like Clarissa? How are you different?

_____

_____

_____

What would you suggest to Clarissa about her relationship with food?

_____

_____

_____

What is your own experience with mindless eating?

_____

_____

_____

_____

## WHAT TO DO

This week, make a date with yourself to eat one meal mindfully, using all your senses to notice what's on the list below. You don't have to do it alone. If you live with others, ask them to join in, too. (This doesn't quite work with infants or very young children, of course!)

First, unplug. No phones, no TV, no music, no devices. Take a deep breath or two. Notice the silence. Notice what's happening in your body and your mind.

Before you even put anything in your mouth, notice the whole meal on the plate; notice the table, the room, the present moment in your home. Then take yourself through the following steps.

1. What does the food look like (appealing, not appealing, color, size)?

2. How does it taste (hot, cold, salty, sweet, sour, spicy, bitter)?

3. What is its texture (crunchy, smooth, creamy, hard)?

4. How does it smell (pungent, mild, pleasant, unpleasant)?

5. What sounds do you notice (fork clanking, apple crunching)?

If eating an entire meal in this way feels like a stretch, start slowly. Just take a few mindful bites of your food. The purpose is to fully experience your food. Record your experience below or download a copy of this worksheet at http://www.newharbinger.com/52762.

What did you eat?

_____

What did it look like?

_____

What did it taste like?

_____

What was its texture?

_____

What did it smell like?

_____

What sounds did you notice?

_____

What did you discover about your relationship to food or to your mealtime habits?

_____

_____

_____

_____

How did you feel doing this exercise? What was positive about it? What was challenging?

_____

_____

_____

What goal(s) would you like to set in the coming weeks to experience more mindful eating? Be specific; for example, "Twice a week, I will eat my lunch mindfully," or "I will eat the first three bites of any meal with mindful awareness."

_____

_____

_____

_____

_____

# 30   Getting Active

*PURPOSE:* To enhance your mind-body connection by doing physical activities you enjoy.

## DID YOU KNOW?

Unless you've been living in a cave for several decades, you're undoubtedly aware that moving your body is good for you—exercise and movement can improve your mood by boosting those pleasure hormones such as endorphins or dopamine. Health benefits include lower blood pressure, better muscle tone, and improved lung capacity.

Some people in recovery fear that, all of a sudden, they have to become gym rats and exercise every day in order to reap the benefits of movement. Those thoughts fall under the category of all-or-nothing thinking and can get in the way of your taking a few simple steps. Literally. Just walking for twenty to thirty minutes a day can improve your mental and physical health. And if that feels daunting at first, start with ten minutes instead.

Maybe you're out of shape. Maybe you were shamed in gym class once. Maybe you are a survivor of trauma and feel so disconnected from your body that you might be afraid to feel what it's like to move. Whatever your experience, it's okay. Start slowly with the methods of integrating movement into your life shown in this exercise. If you continue to have a negative reaction, slow down or stop, and consider consulting a therapist familiar with PTSD and body-held trauma.

## DOES THIS SOUND LIKE YOU?

*Asako, 29, who is recovering from alcohol dependence, is the director of a busy nonprofit and lives by herself. Asako wakes up at 6:00 a.m. and doesn't get home until after her evening SMART Recovery meeting. She worries that she is too sedentary; she suffers from mild depression. When her therapist suggests joining a gym as an incentive to get moving again, Asako says, "Whenever I do that, I go for a week or two and then stop, so why waste the money?"*

How are you like Asako? How are you different?

_____

_____

_____

What do you think Asako could do for physical activity that would fit into her busy life?

_____

_____

_____

_____

# WHAT TO DO

In this exercise, you'll identify some physical activities that you might like to do in the coming weeks and months, either by yourself or with others. Look at this list for some ideas. Add your own.

- Attending aerobics class
- Bicycling
- Dancing
- Doing housework (vacuuming, sweeping, mopping, and so on)
- Fishing
- Gardening
- Golfing
- Jogging
- Playing hockey

- Playing pickleball
- Playing soccer
- Playing softball
- Playing tennis
- Playing volleyball
- Repairing things at home
- Roller-skating
- Running
- Skiing
- Swimming

- Walking
- Washing the car
- Weightlifting
- Yoga
- Other:

_____

_____

_____

_____

_____

Now write down any physical activity that you do now, what you might want to do, and what you used to do in the past. Think about what time of day would be best, how often you want to move, at what intensity level, and for how long. Be realistic. Set small goals so you don't set yourself up for failure. Be sure to consult a physician first, if you have any specific health concerns.

Activities you do now:

_____

_____

New activities you want to do:

_____

_____

Activities you used to do and might want to do again:

_____

_____

What is your goal for the next week?

_____

_____

For the next two weeks?

_____

_____

For the next month?

_____

_____

For the next three months?

_____

_____

What will you need to do to reach those goals (join a gym, ask a friend to be a tennis or pickleball partner, enroll in a yoga class)? Write down your deadline for achieving these goals.

(Example: *I will rejoin my old gym by the first of the month.*)

_____

_____

_____

Keep track of your physical activities on this chart and record your feelings about doing them, either before or after, whichever seems helpful. (Visit http://www.newharbinger.com/52762 for a downloadable version of this worksheet, if you need it.)

| Day | Activity | For how long and at what intensity? | What was it like for you? |
| --- | --- | --- | --- |
|  |  |  |  |
|  |  |  |  |
|  |  |  |  |
|  |  |  |  |
|  |  |  |  |
|  |  |  |  |

# 3I  Your Nutrition and Sleep

*PURPOSE:* To establish healthier eating and sleeping habits by learning and practicing different approaches.

## DID YOU KNOW?

Now that you're taking better care of yourself, it's time to turn to a couple of other elements of the mind-body connection that contribute to a healthy, sober life—nutrition and sleep. In previous exercises, you have been exploring ways to change your relationship to your substance of choice, take steps to prevent relapse, build a supportive network, learn the connection between thoughts and feelings, change your inner dialogue, and increase your level of physical activity. Congratulations on the hard work!

Everyone has different habits for eating and sleep. This section is designed to help you notice in a more mindful way your individual habits and routines, and the consequences of your choices. That is, how are those choices affecting your mind-body connection? Are they helping you in your sobriety or are they slowing down your progress?

## DOES THIS SOUND LIKE YOU?

*Marjorie, 57, a widow, recently attended a ninety-day treatment program for her addiction to alcohol and painkillers that began after her husband died. While at rehab, she regained a sense of her self-worth and hope for the future. During the two-year stretch of her using, she had gained a lot of weight and had irregular sleep patterns. Now that she's home, she wants a fresh start, but she feels overwhelmed and doesn't know where to start.*

How are you like Marjorie? How are you different?

_____

_____

_____

Can you relate to her wish to change some habits but not knowing how to begin? Write your thoughts below.

_____

_____

_____

_____

# WHAT TO DO

As part of your recovery, the best first step you can take is to get a full, proper assessment of all aspects of your physical health, especially if you are planning to make some changes in your eating and/or sleep habits.

## Start with a Medical Checkup

Schedule a physical exam with your primary care doctor, or, if you don't have one, consult with your health insurance plan for a referral. If you've avoided seeing a doctor for a while, here are some things to remember:

- Bring a list of concerns and questions, and don't be afraid to ask about *anything*.

- *Be honest* about any past or current substance use. You've done nothing to be ashamed of, and your doctor should know about all aspects of your health.

- Find out if you are due for any routine preventive exams such as a mammogram, prostate test, colonoscopy, and so on.

- Ask if you need a cholesterol test, complete blood count, urinalysis, thyroid test, blood sugar count, and so on.

Don't forget to schedule a checkup with your dentist, too! Unhealthy teeth and gums can lead to a host of other problems.

## Assess Your Eating Habits

What and when do you eat? Do you eat three meals a day or multiple small meals a day? How often do you snack? Describe a typical day's intake below. Be honest with yourself, without judging.

_____

_____

_____

_____

Do you feel you are at a healthy weight right now? If not, what would you need to do to get to a healthy weight for your body type and height? If you feel you are seriously under- or overweight, you might want to consult with a nutritionist for some extra guidance.

_____

_____

_____

_____

What are your goals concerning your relationship to food? Be specific. Ask for help as needed.

_____

_____

_____

_____

_____

It is important to note that those recovering from problem drinking may have different nutritional needs from someone recovering from opioid or stimulant dependence. Questions of what foods, beverages, and vitamins or supplements to add or subtract from your diet should be decided between you and your doctor or nutritionist. Here are some general ideas for improving your nutrition and eating habits:

- Check with your doctor about your caffeine and soda use.

- Eat regular meals. Try to eat while sitting down, with few or no distractions.

- Eat slowly, both to savor the taste and to help your digestion.

- Choose a good balance of protein, vegetables, healthy carbohydrates, healthy fats, and minimal sugar (if your medical condition allows).

- Drink plenty of water. For more on mindful eating, see exercise 29.

## Assess Your Sleeping Habits

People in recovery, especially early on, may struggle with sleep as their bodies and brains are often readjusting; finding a regular rhythm and sleep-wake pattern can take a while. Ask your doctor about the possible safe use of nonaddictive sleep aids or other natural means of inducing a good night's sleep, such as meditation, relaxation, or soft music.

What is your typical sleep schedule, if any?

_____

_____

How would you evaluate your quality of sleep (poor, satisfactory, good, excellent)?

_____

_____

If your sleep is poor, what have you tried so far? What has worked? Not worked?

_____

_____

What would you want to change about your sleep habits in the short term? In the long term?

_____

_____

Here are some ideas to help you establish a regular, healthy sleep schedule and get better-quality sleep:

- Aim to get into bed around the same time every night.

- Unplug from all electronics at least a half hour before lights-out, if possible.

- Keep the room dark and not too hot or cold.

- Do some gentle stretching or simple yoga before getting into bed.

- Play soothing music or a relaxation recording if you have difficulty falling asleep. (This involves electronics, but it's for a good cause. Don't sneak a peek at Facebook or TikTok!)

- If you wake up in the middle of the night and can't fall back asleep, many people recommend staying in bed to at least rest your body (rather than getting up and doing something). Do a breathing exercise, body scan, grounding exercise, or progressive muscle relaxation exercise.

Now, keep track of your eating- and sleeping-related activities for the following week (or longer if you find it helpful). You can download a worksheet for this exercise at http://www.newharbinger.com/52762.

| Date | Food notes | Sleep notes | Comments |
|------|-----------|-------------|----------|
|      |           |             |          |
|      |           |             |          |
|      |           |             |          |
|      |           |             |          |
|      |           |             |          |
|      |           |             |          |

# 32 Self-Compassion for Shame

*PURPOSE:* To understand how shame shows up in the recovery process and practice self-compassion as an antidote to shame.

## DID YOU KNOW?

As you continue in your recovery, you might be aware of a sense of shame arising—a little or a lot—when you think about your life choices and the consequences of those choices. Your history might weigh on you in certain situations, perhaps as you recall experiences you might have had with friends, colleagues, and, especially, family and loved ones, from the time when you were actively using drugs or alcohol. Or you might feel ashamed now when you feel vulnerable to slips or relapse, as if there is something wrong with you.

What is shame? The American Psychological Association defines shame as "a highly unpleasant self-conscious emotion arising from the sense of there being something dishonorable, immodest, or indecorous in one's own conduct or circumstances." Shame is different from guilt. To paraphrase noted author and social worker Brené Brown (2012): Guilt says, "I made a mistake." Shame says, "I *am* a mistake."

Maybe you're someone who has lived for years with a pervasive sense of shame just for being who you are, long before you started using substances. You are not alone. Some of us grow up with parents or caretakers who actively shamed us with messages that we internalized, like "You're such a loser," "You'll never be good enough," "What is wrong with you?" and the like. Shame is also something we can absorb in response to ethnic, religious, racial, or gender bias or oppression.

All these messages—both internal and external—can add up to a heap of emotional and spiritual pain. And shame can be felt in different intensities at different times: mild to moderate to severe. Whatever the intensity, we can begin to heal the emotion of shame through actively practicing self-compassion, according to psychologist Christopher Germer (2009), a pioneer in this subject. Research has shown that as self-compassion increases, shame decreases (Neff 2023). You can begin today to move in that direction, adding this new tool to your mindful self-compassion toolkit.

## DOES THIS SOUND LIKE YOU?

*Jamie, 32, a graphic designer, is one year free of all substances and enjoying a new, satisfying intimate relationship. At an early age, Jamie identified as nonbinary, that is, neither exclusively male nor female. They had experienced bullying and ridicule because of appearing and acting "different" as a child and teenager. After a slow progression from marijuana to pills to heroin, Jamie decided to take charge of their life and entered a long-term rehab program, where they felt welcomed and accepted. Now that they're physically and mentally clearer, Jamie is recalling some of the shame from the days of active using, including having stolen money from their parents—and trying to reconcile that relationship in the present.*

How are you like Jamie? How are you unlike them?

_____

_____

_____

Have you experienced shame as a result of feeling "different" from others or judged for who you are? Describe.

_____

_____

_____

_____

_____

Have you done or said things in the past that you now understand are part of addictive behaviors and that you feel ashamed about? What are your internal messages about those experiences? Describe.

_____

_____

_____

_____

_____

# WHAT TO DO

**Important!** Working with shame can trigger old, buried feelings of worthlessness or regret, sadness and longing. That is normal and understandable. You may want to just try some parts of this exercise to begin with, see how they go, and come back to the other parts when you are feeling more stable and secure in your sobriety. Be gentle with yourself and stop if it gets too hard. Ask for support as needed. Working with a therapist can be especially useful when it comes to working on shame.

The first step toward self-compassion for shame is mindful awareness—noticing that we're feeling shame while it's happening in the moment. But how can we tell? Here are some common situations when shame can show up:

- A friend or colleague says something that doesn't "land" right with you or makes you feel excluded or misunderstood.

- A family member criticizes, judges, or makes you feel bad about something you've said or done, now or in the past.

- You have an encounter with a stranger that makes you feel uncomfortable, different, or "less than."

- Someone looks at you in a certain way.

- Someone uses a certain tone of voice with you.

- You've made a mistake of some sort (big or little).

- You look in the mirror.

- You are alone and thinking about your future.

- You remember something you did/said when you were actively using.

- You think about certain parts of your childhood.

- You notice something in your environment at home—a photo, an object.

- You notice something out in the world or on TV.

Write down any other situations you can think of here:

_____

_____

_____

_____

_____

*(The following material is drawn from Christopher Germer's "Self-Compassion for Shame" program and used with permission.)*

## Possible Cues for Shame in Daily Life

Put a checkmark next to the items below that ring a bell for you, especially regarding your substance use. Feel free to add your own cues if they're not listed.

**Internal Physical Cues (not visible to others):**

☐ Sinking feeling

☐ Sense of being punched in chest or belly

☐ Tightness in throat or chest

☐ Sense of emptiness in head or heart

☐ Heat flushes or tension in face and jaw

☐ Skin crawling

☐ Nausea

☐ Physical numbness

☐ Other: _____

**External Physical Cues (visible to others):**

☐ Slumping your shoulders

☐ Averting your gaze

☐ Speaking softly

☐ Fidgeting

☐ Freezing, remaining still

☐ Blushing

☐ Swallowing hard

☐ Other: _____

**Mental Cues:**

☐ Confusion: "What is happening?"

☐ Inadequacy: "I'm not good enough."

☐ Self-criticism: "I'm an idiot."

☐ Powerlessness: "What's the point?"

☐ Feeling like an outsider: "I don't fit in."

☐ Vulnerability: "I will be hurt."

☐ Mistrust: "No one is ever here for me."

☐ Worthlessness: "I'm a loser."

☐ Unworthiness: "People won't like me."

☐ Rumination: "Why me?"

☐ Generalization: "I'm always…/never…"

☐ Other: _____

**Emotional Cues:**

☐ Sadness

☐ Anxiety

☐ Fear

☐ Disgust

☐ Irritation

☐ Anger

☐ Emotional numbness

☐ Other: _____

**Behavioral Cues:**

☐ Moving away from a person or situation: shrinking, not speaking, avoiding, disappearing

☐ Moving toward: people pleasing, being submissive or excessively dependent

☐ Moving against: getting angry, being aggressive, shaming others

☐ Other: _____

What do you notice about the items you checked off? Can you identify any patterns? How did it feel to check off those items?

_____

_____

_____

_____

_____

_____

_____

_____

## Skills for Self-Compassion

Now it's time to learn two simple skills to add to your sobriety toolkit. You already have experience noticing certain aspects of your inner and outer world. In step 1, you will focus on noticing shame as it arises; in step 2, you will practice a self-compassion technique designed to alleviate the suffering caused by the experience of shame in daily life.

**Step 1—Keeping Track:** Practice noticing when you are aware of a moment of shame—maybe drawing from the list of situations above. Note that "internal shame," which originates inside the self, involves self-generated criticism and negative self-evaluation. "External shame," which originates outside the self, involves a distressing awareness that others view the self negatively. Try to identify how and where the shame shows up for you (internal, external, emotional, physical, behavioral, etc.), and what the cues and intensity of the cues were. Try it for at least two or three experiences to start. Each time you notice shame, practice making a "compassionate U-turn," as described below. Record your experiences in the chart that follows.

**Step 2—"Compassionate U-Turn":** This exercise is a way to practice giving yourself compassion *in the moment,* as you experience shame. You might want to first imagine what you would say or do to offer kindness and compassion to someone you care about—then do a U-turn to direct those kindnesses to yourself. The goal is not to *get rid of the shame.* The goal is to treat yourself kindly *when you experience shame.* Record your experiences in the chart that follows.

- *Soothing and supportive touch:* If you're comfortable doing so, place your hand over the place on your body where you are experiencing shame. You might massage that part of your body tenderly and gently, as if you were soothing a little child.

- *Kind gaze:* Think of a face, particularly the eyes, of someone you consider deeply compassionate. It could be a friend, a teacher, a grandparent, a parent, child, or a dog or cat you have loved. You can also use the image of someone you don't know whom you believe is loving. Imagine what those eyes and that face look like—imagine they are gazing at you with complete acceptance, love, and kindness. Really let yourself feel the experience.

- *Gentle phrases or calming sounds:* Think of someone who knows you and loves you and accepts you as you are—maybe someone you know or an imaginary person or animal. Now imagine if this person were to lean over and whisper into your ear, softly, gently, something that you need to hear in this moment of feeling shame. What would they say? Maybe "You are okay just as you are," "I love you," "I'm here for you," "I believe in you," or "Everything's going to be okay." Or make up your own statements. Then try saying those words for yourself, toward yourself, repeating them warmly and kindly, as you might with a person or a pet you love or care deeply about.

- *Rest:* After doing your U-turn practice, sit quietly for a few moments if possible, or get a cup of tea or juice, allowing the experience to sink into your body. Take some easy breaths.

## TRACKING SELF-COMPASSION FOR SHAME

| Date/Time | What sparked a sense of shame? What category of shame was it (internal, external, etc.)? | What cues did this experience trigger for you? How did it feel in your body? What thoughts came to mind? | Self-compassionate response | How did you feel then (in your body and mind)? |
|---|---|---|---|---|
| | | | | |
| | | | | |
| | | | | |
| | | | | |

If you would like to continue tracking your practice of self-compassion for shame, visit http://www.newharbinger.com/52762 to download this worksheet.

# 33 Mindful Meditation 101

*PURPOSE:* To quiet your mind and body through practicing formal and informal mindful meditation.

## DID YOU KNOW?

You may remember that *mindfulness* means noticing what is happening right here and now, without judgment and with acceptance. As you continue to learn skills and strategies for sobriety, you might want to add some simple meditation practices.

When some people hear the word *meditation*, they worry that they must subscribe to a certain religious or spiritual belief, or fold themselves into a pretzel and chant. Not so. One of the first people to introduce mindfulness meditation in the West was the late Vietnamese monk and master teacher Thich Nhat Hanh, whose work was deeply anchored in ancient Buddhist traditions. Other well-known masters have offered techniques and practices to people from all walks of life throughout the world, including Insight Meditation Society founders Sharon Salzberg, Jack Kornfield, and Joseph Goldstein; Jon Kabat-Zinn, internationally known teacher and creator of the mindfulness-based stress reduction program; psychologist Tara Brach; and, more recently, author and journalist Dan Harris, among many more.

As mentioned earlier, studies show that even a few minutes of quieting the mind and body on a regular basis can reap big benefits—less depression, less anxiety, lower blood pressure, and improvements in memory and attention. You are training your brain to default to a more relaxed state. That happens only with regular practice. Just as we wouldn't expect a marathon runner to be able to run a race without training, don't expect that you'll immediately reap the benefits of meditation. Slow and steady. One step at a time.

You might want to search for meditation, mindfulness, or guided visualization recordings on YouTube. Sometimes you might want a recording with music, sometimes without. And different voices might be calming to you at different times. Apps such as Calm, Headspace, or Insight Timer are also popular. Explore, experiment, find what works best for you.

There are two categories of mindfulness meditation practices: formal and informal. *Formal practice* refers to intentionally setting aside a period of time each day (or regularly) and sitting (or standing or lying down) quietly. *Informal practice* refers to paying mindful, nonjudgmental attention while doing certain routine daily activities. See the exercise below for more details.

## DOES THIS SOUND LIKE YOU?

*William, 37, a lab technician, stopped smoking marijuana a few months ago when he started dating Monica, who disapproves of any drug use. William likes her and doesn't want to mess up his prospects. After two weeks without marijuana, William feels anxious, restless, and out of sorts. He has heard about mindfulness from Monica, who attends yoga classes and practices meditation. Part of him wants to join her and see what those activities are like. Part of him wants to go back to smoking, as long as he can hide it from Monica.*

How are you like William? How are you different?

_____

_____

_____

Is there a part of you that resists the idea of meditation? Write down your thoughts about this. Or, if you welcome the idea of meditation, write down your thoughts about what you hope or expect.

_____

_____

_____

_____

_____

_____

_____

# WHAT TO DO

*Formal practice* means setting aside a regular time to sit quietly (or lie down, if sitting is uncomfortable) with your eyes closed (or open, gazing steadily downward, if you prefer). The idea is to stop activity, be still, and settle into your body and mind as it is in the present moment. Experts often recommend twenty minutes per day, but if that doesn't work for you, try ten. Or five. Or even start with three. You can always build up over time, just like marathon runners in training.

For your formal meditation practice, find a time when you can eliminate all distractions and unplug from the world. It might be at home or at work; it might be in your car in a parking lot or at your local library. To start, you might choose to repeat a mantra: that is, a word of your choice, such as "peace," "calm," "one," "love," or something that you can use as your anchor when your mind wanders—which it inevitably will.

Don't worry and don't judge. Don't expect that thoughts will magically disappear and you will achieve a blissful "non-thought" state. In fact, the mind is doing what the mind naturally does—generating thoughts. Practice watching the thoughts float past you, like clouds in the sky. *The mindful moment comes when you notice your mind wandering.* Simply bring your attention back to your anchor. You can also use your breath as an anchor, or repeat any of the mindful self-compassion phrases you have developed.

By formally practicing sitting still on a regular basis and simply noticing the flow of thoughts and sensations without judgment and with acceptance, you'll get better at noticing when you are *not* mindful. Again, that "waking up" moment is a moment of mindfulness, pulling you out of your trance and into the present moment. Don't beat yourself up for drifting off; rather, celebrate those moments of awareness!

*Informal practice* refers to paying mindful, nonjudgmental attention while doing certain routine daily activities such as taking a shower, washing the dishes, making the bed, driving, making lunch, going for a walk, and so on.

Start by picking one of the activities mentioned above and see what it is like to pay full attention to what is happening right here and now. For instance, in the shower, do you feel the water on your body? Is it warm enough? Too warm? Do you feel the soap or the shampoo—can you be present throughout the shower? If your mind wanders (for example, to reviewing your to-do list), bring it back to the sensory experience of being in the shower.

This week, try to schedule a few formal meditation sessions and one or two informal practices. During each activity, practice being mindful—noticing how your body feels, noticing your breath, noticing any sensory experiences such as what you see, hear, smell, or touch. Write down your experiences and your responses. (If you need more space, visit http://www.newharbinger.com/52762 for a downloadable version of this worksheet.)

| Day | Formal practice | Response | Informal practice | Response |
|-----|-----------------|----------|-------------------|----------|
| Example: Monday. | Sat for 10 mins. on my couch after work, no phone or TV! Focused on breath. | I liked having something to focus on. I nearly fell asleep! | Paid attention while brushing teeth. | Got fidgety but stuck with it, noticed the fidgetiness, tried not to judge; tasted the minty toothpaste. |
| | | | | |
| | | | | |
| | | | | |

# Look Back and Look Ahead

# 34 Reexamining Your Relationships

*PURPOSE:* To identify those people who will be most supportive of your recovery efforts by analyzing your relationships with family, friends, and others in your network.

## DID YOU KNOW?

Somewhere along the path toward sobriety, most people become more aware of the positives and negatives of their relationships with the people in their lives. If you are in a place in your recovery where you are stabilized medically, trying out new experiences, managing your emotions better, and taking better care of yourself, you might want to take stock of your relationships—past, present, and future—and assess how those relationships have helped you or hurt you, and what to do about them going forward.

## DOES THIS SOUND LIKE YOU?

*Yvonne, 20, is a college student who has struggled with mixed substance use. Although she has stopped using MDMA (ecstasy) and other psychedelics, she still smokes marijuana occasionally. Now she wants to quit that too and see what life is like without mind-altering substances. Yvonne's friends party every Friday night at her friend Katya's house. Katya smokes marijuana and is not planning to stop. When Yvonne asks her to support her goal and not smoke around her, Katya says, "No way. Just because you don't want to smoke doesn't mean the rest of us can't!" Now Yvonne has to decide what to do about her relationship with Katya— to avoid her or hang around her. In the meantime, Yvonne's Uncle Jeff, who used to drink to excess, has invited her to attend AA meetings with him on Friday nights.*

How are you like Yvonne? How are you different?

_____

_____

_____

What do you think Yvonne's best strategy is to support her goal of quitting marijuana?

_____

_____

_____

_____

# WHAT TO DO

Take this empowering opportunity to look back and look ahead. In this exercise, you'll identify the most important people in your life, past and present, in the following categories: family, friends, coworkers/fellow students, and community.

On the lines below, list the people with whom you have close relationships and identify them by category. For example, Yvonne's list would include Katya (friend) and Uncle Jeff (family), and so on. The goal is to assess for yourself which people you believe will be supportive of your ongoing recovery and which people might interfere with your positive growth and whom you might need to let go of or back away from.

_____   _____

_____   _____

_____   _____

_____   _____

_____   _____

_____   _____

_____   _____

Next, fill in the following chart and answer these questions:

1.  How often do you have contact with this person?

2.  On a scale from 1 to 10 (1 = not at all, 5 = somewhat, 10 = extremely), how supportive is this person of your substance-use recovery goals?

3.  What is your goal for this relationship? (Keep it as is? See more of this person? See them less?)

4.  Note the reason for your stated goal.

Take your time with this exercise. It doesn't need to be done all in one sitting. You might start filling it in and then come back to it over time, as you see fit. (If you need more space, you'll find a worksheet for this exercise at http://www.newharbinger.com/52762.)

| Name | Relationship | Frequency of involvement? | Level of support (1–10) | Your goal for this relationship | Reasons for your goal |
|---|---|---|---|---|---|
| Example: Katya | College friend | Daily | 1 | Keep friendship for now, but tell her I can't hang out on Fridays. | She smokes daily; doesn't respect my choices. |
| Example: Uncle Jeff | Dad's brother | 2-3x/month | 10 | See more often—go to Friday meetings! | He knows my story and could be helpful. |
| | | | | | |
| | | | | | |
| | | | | | |
| | | | | | |

# 35 Dear Self...Yes, You! Part II

*PURPOSE:* To enhance your sense of self-empowerment and prevent relapse by continuing your dialogue with the different parts of yourself.

## DID YOU KNOW?

Earlier in this workbook, you identified the parts of yourself we called the wise self and the addicted self (see exercise 5). As you progress in your recovery, you may have noticed that your inner dialogue has changed (see exercise 23). Perhaps you're more patient and compassionate with yourself. Perhaps you're better able to manage urges and cravings by identifying the automatic thoughts that precede an action or behavior. Perhaps your addicted self is no longer calling the shots. Congratulations!

Somewhere between your wise self and your addicted self is a voice we'll call your *recovering self*. This part of you likely goes back and forth, back and forth. This part might not have instant access to that longed-for wisdom, but it's trying hard and is open to encouragement and validation. Getting in touch with what your recovering self has to say can broaden your self-understanding and strengthen your commitment to building a healthier, happier life.

## DOES THIS SOUND LIKE YOU?

*Alice, 40, a self-employed artist with a history of opiate dependence, has worked on identifying the voices of her wise self and addicted self by listening mindfully and without judgment, writing down her inner dialogue, and talking with her therapist about her struggles. She has been drug-free for thirty days but says her confidence is getting shaky. Her therapist encouraged her to write down what her wise self might have to say to her recovering self at this stage.*

How are you like Alice? How are you different?

_____

_____

_____

What might Alice's recovering self have to say if she could give it a voice?

_____

_____

_____

_____

_____

_____

What might Alice's wise self want to say to her recovering self?

_____

_____

_____

_____

_____

_____

# WHAT TO DO

First, go back and look at your "Dear Self, Part I" letter (exercise 5), which gave voice to your wise self and addicted self. What do you notice when you read that now? What has changed? What is the same?

_____

_____

_____

_____

_____

_____

What would you add to that conversation now?

_____

_____

_____

_____

_____

Now, let's zero in on your recovering self. Below are some examples of what that part of you might be saying. Use the blank lines that follow to write down some of the familiar phrases that come to mind when you pay attention to what your recovering self has to say.

Examples:

- "I know what I should do, but part of me wants to give up. This is so hard! Sometimes I wonder what the whole point of sobriety is."

- "My partner urged me to stop drinking, so I did. It's been a few months now. I've proved to her that I can do it. I'm in control. Obviously, I don't have an addiction. So maybe I can drink once in a while after all."

- "It's hard not to use when everyone around me seems to be doing it. I do feel so much better about myself now, but sometimes I feel sorry for myself, too."

_____

_____

_____

_____

_____

_____

_____

_____

_____

Now, write a short letter from your wise self to your recovering self. Use extra paper if needed. What wisdom does your wise self want to offer your recovering self? In what ways can your wise self listen to and reassure your recovering self that they are on the right path? Do the best you can. There's no right or wrong. Writing a letter like this can open up some insights into what your subconscious mind might be thinking and feeling, which can lead to making sober choices.

Dear Recovering Self,

_____

_____

_____

_____

_____

_____

_____

_____

_____

_____

_____

_____

_____

_____

_____

_____

_____

# 36 What Are Your Strengths?

*PURPOSE:* To increase your self-confidence and motivation by identifying and rating your emotional strengths.

## DID YOU KNOW?

It's hard to feel good about yourself and tap into your positive qualities when you are in the throes of problem substance use or addiction. As we discussed in exercise 32, guilt, shame, and self-doubt are extremely common emotions among people in recovery. Even if you've been doing well, those residual, self-critical feelings, perhaps deeply ingrained from long before your addiction began, tend to hang around.

As you continue growing and changing, it is essential that you connect—perhaps for the first time ever, or for the first time in a long time—with the positive aspects of yourself. Knowing you have strengths, believing in yourself, and nurturing relationships with others who value you and your strengths are key to a sober life.

## DOES THIS SOUND LIKE YOU?

*In group therapy, Stephen, 48, a married father of two adult children, is working on his longstanding alcohol dependence. He has relapsed frequently and continually puts himself down: "Let's face it. I'm a drunk. There. I said it. I've tried so many times to be a good person, but I always fail." When asked to share a couple of things that he thinks are strengths, Stephen hesitates. "I have no idea. It's been so long since I felt good about myself."*

How are you like Stephen? How are you different?

_____

_____

_____

What might you say to Stephen if you were in a support group together?

_____

_____

_____

_____

What are your feelings about trying to identify your emotional strengths? Does it make you feel excited and hopeful? Or does it make you feel nervous or worried that you might not come up with anything? Describe below.

_____

_____

_____

_____

_____

# WHAT TO DO

Below you'll find a list of statements that reflect important emotional strengths. Rate each statement from 1 to 10, with 1 = strongly disagree and 10 = strongly agree.

_____ I am able to love other people.

_____ My self-esteem is usually high.

_____ I am a flexible person.

_____ I am a creative person.

_____ I am a curious person.

_____ I don't let other people's opinions of me keep me from doing what I think is right.

_____ I am assertive when it comes to looking after my own interests and the interests of those I care about.

_____ I set realistic goals for myself.

_____ I have good common sense.

_____ I am able to control my impulses.

_____ I take care of my body and my health.

_____ I am a flexible person.

_____ I usually trust other people.

_____ I would not describe myself as a victim.

_____ I don't have a problem dealing with things that are unknown or uncertain.

_____ I am easygoing most of the time.

_____ I keep calm even when I am stressed.

_____ I am patient.

_____ I am a positive thinker.

_____ I take responsibility for my decisions and actions.

_____ I am well-liked.

_____ I enjoy the company of others and also enjoy being alone.

_____ I am good at predicting other people's behavior.

_____ I am self-aware and like to learn about myself.

_____ If something is bothering me, I can usually figure out what it is and do something about it.

_____ My sense of humor often helps me deal with stress.

_____ If I can't control a certain situation, I can usually stop my worried thoughts.

_____ I have several close people I can confide in.

_____ When I need help, I have several people I can turn to.

_____ I have a strong support network.

_____ I don't have a problem getting angry when it is warranted.

_____ I have techniques I use to calm myself down when I am upset.

_____ I accept my feelings, even when they sometimes trouble me.

_____ I am able to talk openly and honestly when something is bothering me.

_____ When I make a mistake, I try to figure out what I did wrong and learn from it.

List any other emotional strengths that come to mind:

_____

_____

_____

_____

_____

Review your list of emotional strengths. Pick one or two and describe below an incident that demonstrates how you used this strength to address a problem in your life.

_____

_____

_____

_____

What would a caring family member say is your greatest strength?

_____

_____

_____

What would your best friend say is your greatest strength?

_____

_____

_____

What is an emotional strength that helps you in your relationships?

_____

_____

_____

Describe the best parts of your personality in five words:

_____

_____

_____

_____

_____

# 37 What Are Your Passions?

*PURPOSE:* To move forward in your recovery by identifying the things in life that you are most passionate about.

## DID YOU KNOW?

What do you think of when you hear the word "passion"? Do you think of sex? Romance? Feeling ecstatic? Or do you think of being out of control? Overly emotional? Something else? The concept of passion doesn't always conjure up positive feelings for people in recovery. Passion typically implies having and expressing strong emotions—and that's not always easy for people struggling with addiction.

But feeling passionate doesn't necessarily mean you're bouncing around with glee all day long. Passion can be a quiet emotion, like having a deep-down sense of joy and satisfaction. It doesn't even have to be shared if you don't want to.

As you move along in your recovery process, getting back in touch with, or identifying for the first time, what you are passionate about—what really floats your boat or gets you out of bed in the morning—can give you the boost of motivation you need to continue on your path toward a happier, healthier life.

## DOES THIS SOUND LIKE YOU?

*Harold, 27, is an unemployed college graduate in recovery from longtime heroin addiction. He now attends a methadone clinic in his community and has been stabilized on the medication for six months. He is making new, supportive connections in the recovery community and attending Narcotics Anonymous meetings daily. His NA sponsor suggested that he think about applying for a part-time job in the near future doing something that he is passionate about, which makes Harold anxious. "I have no idea what I want to do or what I'm passionate about. Since I was using for most of my twenties, I feel lost. I don't know who I really am."*

How are you like Harold? How are you different?

_____

_____

_____

Can you relate to Harold's sense of not knowing who he is? If so, in what ways?

_____

_____

_____

_____

What might be some obstacles Harold will face as he tries to figure out what he is passionate about? What would you want to say to Harold to encourage him?

_____

_____

_____

_____

# WHAT TO DO

These questions are designed to get you thinking about your own passions. It's okay to skip around and answer the ones that have the most relevance and meaning for you. Describe on a separate piece of paper or in your journal how the information you've learned might help you move forward in your recovery.

What are a few things that get you excited—things you love talking and thinking about?

_____

_____

Name three or four things that you loved to do as a child.

_____

_____

What jobs or careers make you think, *Wow, I wish I could do that!?*

_____

_____

Do you know anyone in that career? Or someone who might know someone? List them here.

_____

_____

What talents do you have (for example, music, art, writing, building things, fixing things, athletics)?

_____

_____

What would other people (friends, family, teachers) say you're talented at?

_____

_____

Imagine you're at the end of your life, looking back. What are one or two things you absolutely need to do or create so that you can say you fulfilled your potential?

_____

_____

If money were no object and you could work for free, what would be your dream job?

_____

_____

If you had to give a talk, write a book, or make a video about something you are passionate and knowledgeable about, what would the topic be?

_____

_____

What would bring you a sense of fulfillment and perhaps even contribute to the world?

_____

_____

What activity would keep you so totally engaged that you wouldn't notice if hours passed?

_____

_____

If money were no object and you could go back to school to study anything you want to learn more about, what would it be?

_____

_____

If a doctor told you that you had less than a year to live, what would you drop everything to do right away?

_____

_____

What do you want to be doing that would make you really happy?

_____

_____

What would be worth giving up drugs and alcohol for if you could be guaranteed success and happiness in a certain career?

_____

_____

# 38 HOPE Is in the Air

*PURPOSE:* To maintain your momentum in addiction recovery by learning the HOPE model.

## DID YOU KNOW?

You wouldn't be reading this workbook if at least a little part of you didn't believe things could get better. Without hope, it's hard to get through the inevitable setbacks and failures. Without hope, it's hard to create a vision of the future and set goals for yourself that will result in less stress and more satisfaction.

In this exercise, you'll work with an acronym, HOPE, which stands for **H**ealing, **O**penness, **P**atience, and **E**xpectations. Naming and working with these four wonderful aspects of life—and of your ongoing recovery—can enhance your sense of well-being and keep you on the path to successful sobriety.

**Healing.** Do we ever truly heal 100 percent, like how a scrape or cut eventually heals over and there's no scar whatsoever? Probably not. There will always be the experience of the wound. But we can work *toward* healing from life's difficulties with a mindful attitude and self-compassion.

People in recovery from addiction have frequently suffered terribly in their lives: childhood traumas such as abuse, neglect, bullying, losses, divorce, living with a mentally ill family member, or living with someone with an active addiction. Many have experienced oppression or "-isms" such as racism, classism, or sexism. With good therapy and a lot of support, your adult self can understand and accept those wounds. You can learn to say, "That happened to me. It wasn't my fault. I have skills now for taking care of myself and moving on."

Trauma experts talk about how our wounds are stored in our body and mind and can affect us for the rest of our lives if they are not dealt with. You deserve to heal. You deserve to take the time to make a new relationship with your past. This doesn't necessarily mean forgiving those who have wounded you; this means *forgiving yourself* in the present, acknowledging that you've done the best you can, and moving toward a new, more fulfilling future.

**Openness.** Most of us, when we're wounded or hurting, want to protect ourselves from further harm. That makes sense. So how do we ever experience anything new if we stay in our bubble? Remember the earlier exercise "Stretching Out of Your Comfort Zone" (exercise 15)? It takes a leap of faith to try something new or break an old habit. Yes, there is a risk, but what things in life that are good and wonderful don't involve some kind of risk? With an open mind, an open heart, and an open spirit, you can add riches to your life that you might never have dreamed of—a sense of safety, strength, control, happiness, respect, love, and connection. Those are yours for the asking.

**Patience.** *What do you mean, mine for the asking?* you might wonder. *I've been wanting good stuff in my life for as long as I can remember!* That's where patience comes in handy. It can't be said enough: Change can be hard. Change can be slow. Seeing the fruits of your efforts, especially if you're someone who craves instant gratification, can take time.

Be patient with that urgency. Listen to it and acknowledge it—don't push it away, because it can add positive, driving energy to your journey. Use your mindfulness skills to watch your thoughts come and go, and invest every day in your recovery activities so that you can set the stage for getting what you want.

**Expectations.** Here's another dilemma. You might ask, "What if I work on healing, acknowledge my wounds with compassion, practice patience with the nature of change, and my life is still stressful and unmanageable sometimes?"

Welcome to reality. That statement isn't meant to be cynical or punitive. It's just true. We don't always get our way. Most things in life are out of our control. It can be frustrating, but it can also be freeing to realize that we can dream and plan and set goals and have the process be rewarding, without necessarily having all of our expectations fulfilled.

So even if you work hard and do all the right things, you might not achieve the "perfect" life. And "perfect" is an illusion, anyway. Shoot for good enough. Shoot for okay for today. Shoot for being grateful in the moment for what you do have. HOPE is a process. Embrace it as best as you can.

## DOES THIS SOUND LIKE YOU?

Often, when we're in recovery, it can be hard to figure out what to do when new opportunities arise. Are we ready for them? Read about Penny's situation below.

*Penny, a divorced woman who works as a medical technician at a large hospital, is about to turn forty. She recently attended a four-week intensive outpatient program (IOP) following detox for alcohol dependence. She is proud of herself for being honest with her family, friends, and employers, and excited about turning forty and "starting my life over again." In the IOP, she met a divorced man who is also in early recovery. They hit it off and got together for coffee a few times on the outside. They are very attracted to each other and, for both, it's been a long time since they've been in a relationship. But Penny worries that it might be too soon to manage both her own recovery and a new boyfriend.*

How are you like Penny? How are you different?

_____

_____

_____

How would you assess Penny's situation? List some pros and cons.

_____

_____

_____

_____

_____

What parts of the HOPE approach might be helpful for Penny at this time?

_____

_____

_____

_____

_____

# WHAT TO DO

In this exercise, you will have the chance to explore each aspect of the HOPE model. But first, write down your response to this overall question: What are your hopes?

Here are some examples to get you thinking:

- "I hope I can maintain my focus on myself and not back down from setting limits with others."

- "I hope I will find a great job in an area I'm passionate about."

- "I hope I can regain my parents' (spouse's/partner's/children's/friends') trust if I continue to work hard."

Now it's your turn. What are your hopes?

_____

_____

_____

_____

Next, answer the following questions under each category. Focus on how you're feeling about each aspect of HOPE *today*. You can always come back to these questions at a later date and add to your responses.

## Healing

What wounds are you carrying from your past that need to be healed?

_____

_____

_____

_____

What people could help you in your healing process?

_____

_____

_____

_____

What activities or recovery strategies could help you in your healing process?

_____

_____

_____

_____

Are you willing to experience some emotional discomfort without picking up drugs or alcohol? Why or why not? Which skills that you've learned would help you solidify your sobriety during periods of emotional discomfort?

_____

_____

_____

_____

If your answer to the last question was no, or if you felt ambivalence or other feelings coming up that you might want help to work through, consider seeing a therapist or another helping professional, if you aren't already. It's absolutely normal to feel ambivalence, and asking for help and support is always a strong, sober choice.

## Openness

Do you think of yourself as a closed or open person, or somewhere in between? Explain.

_____

_____

_____

_____

_____

Do you remember a time when you felt open to change and new experiences? Describe.

_____

_____

_____

_____

_____

Who or what inspires you to remain open, maybe even to feel vulnerable, in the interest of leaving your comfort zone?

_____

_____

_____

_____

_____

What are you willing to do in the coming weeks and months to practice being more open to new people, places, and things?

_____

_____

_____

_____

_____

## Patience

How would you rate your ability to be patient? _____ (1 = low ability, 5 = moderate ability, 10 = excellent ability)

Do you remember a time when you were forced to be patient, waiting for something good? Describe it.

_____

_____

_____

_____

_____

What would you be willing to wait for now, and what could you say to yourself to learn more patience?

_____

_____

_____

_____

_____

## Expectations

What are your expectations of yourself regarding your recovery right now?

_____

_____

_____

_____

What are your expectations of others regarding your recovery? Be specific.

_____

_____

_____

_____

How do you manage having unmet expectations (being disappointed)? Be specific.

_____

_____

_____

_____

_____

How would you like to manage having unmet expectations?

_____

_____

_____

_____

_____

Are you setting your expectations too high, too low, or just right? Describe two or three experiences that illustrate your answer.

_____

_____

_____

_____

_____

_____

_____

# 39 Vision Statement, Part II

*PURPOSE:* To continue generating a sense of hope by creating a vision of what you'd like your life to look like in five years and ten years.

## DID YOU KNOW?

In exercise 2, you had the opportunity to create a vision statement for your future. To do an exercise like this might seem contrary to the popular phrase used in AA "One day at a time." You might say, "Who knows what the future holds? If everything is out of our control, why not just let things unfold?"

Sure, that makes sense. But no one is saying that the vision statement is some kind of contract. Rather, it is an expression of parts of yourself that you might have hidden away or buried for years—the parts that want a happy, healthy, fulfilling life. It can't hurt to envision that for yourself, can it? Having a goal or vision is an important element of motivation that can keep you going during rough times and enhance your pleasure in the good times.

## DOES THIS SOUND LIKE YOU?

*Vincent, 26, has stopped drinking alcohol and smoking marijuana after getting off probation following a series of DUIs. He won't get his license back for another six months. He is living at home with his parents and recently got a "recovery" job (a minimally demanding job) bagging groceries while he attends court-ordered SMART Recovery meetings and individual and group therapy a few times a week. For the moment, Vincent is motivated to stick to the terms of his probation. When a group leader asks him about his hopes for the future, he says he can't possibly imagine what his life will look like five and ten years from now. He doesn't even know what he'll be doing next month.*

How are you like Vincent? How are you different?

_____

_____

_____

Are you aware of anything—internal or external—that might be in the way of your working toward what you want? Describe it briefly.

_____

_____

_____

_____

_____

_____

## WHAT TO DO

In this exercise, you'll create another vision statement to help you keep your eyes on the prize—that is, living a happier life.

Go back and look at your "Dear Self" letters in exercises 5 and 35. Review your strengths, your passions, and your HOPE answers in exercises 36–38. Then relax. Maybe even meditate for a few minutes. Allow yourself to dream.

Then, review your list of twelve things that you want in your life from your first vision statement. Now, add twelve more. Use extra paper if needed. As before, you may create a collage of images from magazines or download photos or images from the internet.

**Things I Want in My Life:**

1. _____

2. _____

3. _____

4. _____

5. _____

6. _____

7. _____

8. _____

9. _____

10. _____

11. _____

12. _____

Now, you'll create another vision statement. This time, focus on your vision for five and ten years from now. As before, here are some categories you might want to include:

- Relationship to drugs and/or alcohol

- Relationships with friends

- Relationships with family

- Intimate relationships

- Health

- Finances

- Job/school

- Spirituality

As before, the key is to write in the present tense, pretending it is five years, then ten years from now. Here is Vincent's five-year vision statement:

*"I did it! I haven't had a drink or smoked weed in five years. I can't believe it! Never in a million years, in the early days, did I think I could do it. I figured I would relapse, like always. But I did what I was advised to do—dumped my old friends who were using, saw a great therapist, joined a support group, and worked on my self-care. I haven't been in any legal trouble and feel much better about myself. It wasn't always easy, but I kept myself focused on my goal: to go back and complete my college degree. I have a different part-time job now to help support my school expenses, and I live in an apartment with other sober guys. I'm thinking about helping other people who have had problems with drugs and alcohol. Who knows? Maybe I'll even become a counselor myself."*

## My Five-Year Vision Statement

_____

_____

_____

_____

_____

_____

_____

_____

_____

_____

_____

_____

_____

## My Ten-Year Vision Statement

_____

_____

_____

_____

_____

_____

_____

_____

_____

_____

_____

_____

# Wrapping Up

Congratulations! You've come to the end of this workbook. Maybe you've dipped into a few, or a lot, of the exercises presented here. Maybe you've completed them all. Whatever your pace and process has been, I hope you've not only gained insight into your problem substance use and its roots but also expanded your awareness of your true self, your thoughts, your feelings, your relationships, your vulnerabilities, and your strengths—and learned helpful skills along the way. Starting a sober life is an act of courage involving some losses, yes, but so many more gains. Feel free to come back to this book and work with the daily exercises and the online activities at any time. Remember to celebrate your accomplishments! And, always, be kind to yourself.

# Daily Exercises

The following four exercises are designed to be used every day or as often as you wish. You may photocopy these pages or download them at http://www.newharbinger.com/52762.

# Today's Goal

Setting daily goals can be an important part of maintaining good sobriety. Goals can give you something to dream about and work toward. Meeting your goals, whether small or large, can give you a sense of pride, accomplishment, and accountability.

Keep it simple. Maybe one day you set a goal of making a phone call to an old friend. Perhaps another day you set a goal of going to the gym for an hour or taking a walk in nature. Here are some categories that you might want to set a goal for:

- Attending a social event
- Completing one mindfulness activity
- Connecting with a loved one (phone, text, in person)
- Doing one recovery activity
- Doing something creative
- Doing something spiritual (prayer, religious gathering)

- Eating mindfully
- Exercising
- Getting away for the day
- Meeting a friend
- Relaxing
- Add your own:

_____

Morning: What is today's goal? What do I need to do to meet this goal?

_____
_____
_____
_____
_____

Evening: Did I meet my goal? Why or why not? How do I feel about today's goal?

_____
_____
_____
_____
_____

# What Are Your Challenges?

At the end of each day, you might feel burdened by worries about the future, unfinished business, upcoming stressful events, or your own inner uncertainty about how you're doing and where your recovery work is leading. Writing down one or two challenges daily will help you get out of your head and into some healthy problem solving using the skills you've learned.

On the lines below, identify one or two challenges you face for tomorrow. First, state what the challenge is. Then, write down how you feel about it and what you think you can do to meet it. Finally, tomorrow, note whether you met your goal and how you feel about it. Here's an example:

**Challenge:** I'm going to a work event tomorrow where I know alcohol will be served.

**Feelings before:** Anxious. I might be triggered to drink.

**What can I do?** Tell a friend that I need support; call sponsor before and after; take three conscious breaths. If I can't deal, I'll leave.

**How did it go?** Yesterday, I told a friend, called my sponsor after (not before); forgot to do the breathing. Stayed long enough to connect with people. Drank soda water. Left early.

**Feelings after:** Happy I didn't drink! Friend and sponsor were supportive. Will work on the breathing exercise next time.

**Challenge 1:** _____

**Feelings before:** _____

**What can I do?** _____

**How did it go?** _____

**Feelings after:** _____


**Challenge 2:** _____

**Feelings before:** _____

**What can I do?** _____

**How did it go?** _____

**Feelings after:** _____

# What Are You Grateful For?

Research shows that expressing gratitude is a balm for depression, fear, worry, and anxiety. At the end of each day, identify up to five things you're grateful for. Your choices can be simple, such as running water, electricity, a roof over your head, your safe neighborhood, your pet, and so on. Or you might want to list specific things like "My boss said kind things to me today," or "My partner brought me flowers," or "I felt clearheaded and positive today." Keep up this daily practice for at least three weeks. Notice any subtle changes in your mood or attitude about what's "really important" in life. Practicing gratitude can be a powerful experience. Enjoy!

Date: _____

List five things you are grateful for today:

1. _____

   _____

2. _____

   _____

3. _____

   _____

4. _____

   _____

5. _____

   _____

# The Big Brag

Yes. This is exactly what it sounds like. You are invited to brag, and make it big, bold, and beautiful. How often do we ever get to pound our chests like proud gorillas and say, "Behold, world! Look what I have done!"?

Write down something you did or said today that made you feel really good about yourself; for example, "I cooked an amazing lasagna, and everyone complimented me," or "I talked to my friend who has been hurtful to me and told her how I felt," or "I took a plane trip and could have had a drink without anyone knowing—but I didn't," or "I was finally honest with my doctor," or "I spoke at a meeting." Your big brag doesn't have to be recovery related, but it's fine if it is. Don't be modest. This is your moment to shine.

Date: _____

Write down your big brag of the day. Don't hold back! Celebrate yourself!

_____

_____

_____

_____

_____

_____

_____

_____

_____

_____

_____

_____

_____

_____

# Acknowledgments

I want to express my deep gratitude to the following people, who helped make this workbook possible: Lawrence Shapiro at Between Sessions Resources for inviting me to write the first edition. New Harbinger's Jess O'Brien for championing the new edition; Vicraj Gill for her wise and thoughtful edits; Amy Shoup for the gorgeous cover design; Michele Waters and the entire production team for their patience and skill. Jean Blomquist, copyeditor extraordinaire, for sweating the small stuff as much as I do, with grace and humor. Mitch Abblett, Mark Albanese, Tara Brach, Patrick Griswold, Jan Kauffman, Michael Otto, Larry Peltz, and Chris Willard for their generous endorsements. My brother, Donald Sosin, for composing and performing the relaxing music on the audio recordings. Chris Willard for his enthusiastic support and for facilitating the New Harbinger connection. Chris Germer for writing the foreword, for his wisdom and compassion, and for being a guiding light in my life. Finally, my courageous clients, whose willingness to embrace change has inspired me beyond measure.

# Additional Resources

## Getting Professional Help

The professional treatment of problem substance use and addiction can range from acute medical intervention to less intensive outpatient programs. A trained professional can help you assess your best options. Most programs are covered by health insurance, but some require self-pay. Please check with your employer and/or insurance company, if applicable, to find out about your mental health and substance-use benefits.

### MENTAL HEALTH EVALUATION

People with problem substance use often suffer from underlying, and often untreated, psychiatric or psychological problems such as depression, anxiety, PTSD, bipolar disorder, ADHD, and so on. If you suspect, or if you have been told, that you have a co-occurring disorder, please consult with a mental health professional for a thorough evaluation. In addition, people with substance-use problems have often experienced adversity during childhood: abuse, neglect, exposure to violence, bullying, parental divorce, racism, and so on. Sorting out the variables of your particular history will be important to your recovery.

### MEDICATION EVALUATION

Depending on your medical status, you might seek an evaluation for medication to support your recovery, including FDA-approved medications that have been shown to be very effective in reducing cravings and/or blocking the effects of substances. These medications include buprenorphine, methadone, naloxone, naltrexone, and Suboxone (a combination of buprenorphine and naloxone) for opiate dependence. Medications that help people with alcohol dependence may include disulfiram, acamprosate, and naltrexone, among others. Please consult with an experienced, compassionate specialist in addictions to find out if medication is an appropriate treatment for you.

### INPATIENT DETOX

These hospital- or clinic-based programs are for clients who require medical attention to treat the dangerous and/or uncomfortable physical effects of withdrawal from alcohol and/or drugs such as benzodiazepines (for example, Xanax, Klonopin, Valium, or Ativan) or opiates (for example, heroin, fentanyl, Oxycodone, Vicodin, or Percocet). The length of an inpatient detox program is usually short—from twenty-four hours to a few days.

# RESIDENTIAL TREATMENT/REHAB

In these rehabilitation programs, clients live on-site at a treatment facility, usually for twenty-eight or thirty days (sometimes for sixty or ninety days or more). They attend groups and individual therapy during the day and, often, self-help meetings off-site.

# DAY TREATMENT (INTENSIVE OUTPATIENT/IOP)

Most day treatment programs, or IOPs, are offered at hospital-based settings. Many run five days a week during the day for two or three weeks, and sometimes longer. Some clients go from long-term rehab or hospitalization to an IOP as a "step-down" model of gaining ongoing support and skills training. Since the pandemic, some IOPs have become available virtually. Ask your health care provider about such options.

# OUTPATIENT TREATMENT

Less-intensive outpatient addictions treatment options can range from once-weekly individual psychotherapy in an office or clinic setting to a combination of individual therapy and one or more group therapy meetings per week. (Again, check out virtual options that might be available.) Some programs also require (or suggest) family meetings. Family therapy or family members' participation in Al-Anon or similar programs can be a crucial part of one's recovery. Parents, spouses, and children are deeply affected when a family member is struggling with drug or alcohol use. When loved ones learn facts and strategies to deal with a recovering family member, everyone benefits.

# MINDFULNESS-BASED RELAPSE PREVENTION (MBRP)

Another group approach to addiction recovery was developed by psychologists Sarah Bowen, Neha Chawla, and G. Alan Marlatt at the Addictive Behaviors Research Center at the University of Washington. The program draws from the practice and philosophies of mindfulness and mindfulness-based cognitive therapy to address relapse prevention, primarily as an aftercare treatment for people who want to maintain their progress and learn more about the mind-body connection. There is no requirement for abstinence from using substances.

# PSYCHEDELIC-ASSISTED PSYCHOTHERAPY (PAP)

Although still considered controversial, PAP for addiction recovery is gaining more attention and acceptance. As of this writing, most psychedelic drugs are still illegal under federal laws, except in Oregon and cities such as Denver, Colorado, and Santa Cruz, California, where psychedelics have been decriminalized. PAP involves in-person sessions with trained professionals who administer drugs such as MDMA (ecstasy), psilocybin, or ketamine in a controlled clinical environment. Early studies indicate that psilocybin, the active ingredient in psychedelic mushrooms, can be helpful for those who have been diagnosed with alcohol use disorders, among other substances. But there are downsides: PAP sessions can last up to eight hours and are rarely covered by health insurance, so treatment can be costly. Legal access and concerns about misuse and adverse reactions remain an important factor.

# Finding Self-Help Programs

One of the greatest markers of success in recovery is being connected to a group, a community, or a team of supporters—people who truly understand the unique challenges of problem drug and alcohol use. Self-help groups are powerful, accessible resources to help people feel less isolated and more motivated to change.

## TWELVE-STEP PROGRAMS

**Alcoholics Anonymous (AA), Cocaine Anonymous (CA), Marijuana Anonymous (MA), or Narcotics Anonymous (NA)**

Most people are familiar with the AA model of recovery, which emphasizes total abstinence from mind-altering substances. It is a free group program that is available worldwide, in person and online, and includes twelve specific steps toward recovery. The AA (or CA, MA, NA) model emphasizes that addiction is a disease. AA also has a spiritual basis, offering the idea of asking God or a higher power for help and encouraging members to "surrender" or "let go" in order to break free from the compulsion to use. Meetings offer a safe, anonymous fellowship, where attendees can hear about others' experiences and share their own, if desired. There are different types of meetings, including open vs. closed, beginners, 12-step, or Big Book Study, as well as demographic-specific meetings such as those for women, men, teens, families, BIPOC (Black, indigenous, and/or people of color), LGBTQIA+, and so on. Members can ask for a sponsor, that is, someone also recovering from addiction who is sober.

## SMART RECOVERY

SMART stands for Self-Management and Recovery Training and draws on theories and strategies from cognitive behavioral psychology. People are taught skills to understand how their thoughts and feelings influence their choices and how they can learn to make better choices about addictive behaviors in general. Free meetings facilitated by volunteers are offered worldwide, in person and online.

## SOBER CURIOUS

New trends aimed at helping people cut back or moderate substance use are growing in popularity, especially among health-conscious millennials and Gen Zers. The Sober Curious movement, which includes Dry January and Sober October, is an opportunity for people to think more mindfully about the consequences of substance use in their lives and perhaps make different choices. Some might choose total abstinence during a designated period. Others might experiment with other behavior changes such as declining a drink at a party, sponsoring an alcohol-free event, hosting a sober Super Bowl viewing party, and so on.

> **Note:** For those with chemical dependency, quitting "cold turkey" can be medically dangerous and lead to seizures, hallucinations, or death. The safest plan is to check with your doctor first.

# Words of Wisdom

Alcoholics Anonymous and other 12-step programs are well known for their simple but powerful phrases to help people stay on track. Here are some helpful ones for you to reflect on, write down, put on your phone, or say aloud:

# References

Brown, B. 2012. *Daring Greatly: How the Courage to Be Vulnerable Transforms the Way We Live, Love, Parent, and Lead.* New York: Avery Publishing.

Germer, C. K. 2009. *The Mindful Path to Self-Compassion: Freeing Yourself from Destructive Thoughts and Emotions.* New York: Guilford Press.

Greenfield, S. 2015. *Mind Change: How Digital Technologies Are Leaving Their Mark on Our Brains.* New York: Random House.

National Institute on Drug Abuse (NIDA). 2022, March 22. "Drugs and the Brain." http://nida.nih.gov/publications/drugs-brains-behavior-science-addiction/drugs-brain.

Neff, K. D. 2003. "Self-Compassion: An Alternative Conceptualization of a Healthy Attitude Toward Oneself." *Self and Identity* 2: 85–102.

———. 2023. "Self-Compassion: Theory, Method, Research, and Intervention." *Annual Review of Psychology* 74: 193–218.

Neff, K. D., and C. K. Germer. 2013. "A Pilot Study and Randomized Controlled Trial of the Mindful Self-Compassion Program." *Journal of Clinical Psychology* 69(1): 28–44.

Prochaska J. O., C. DiClemente, and J. C. Norcross. 1992. "In Search of How People Change: Applications to Addictive Behaviors." *American Psychologist* 47(9): 1102–1114.

Prochaska, J. O., W. F. Velicer, J. S. Rossi, M. G. Goldstein, B. H. Marcus, W. Rakowski, C. Fiore, et al. 1994. "Stages of Change and Decisional Balance for 12 Problem Behaviors." *Health Psychology* 13(1): 39–46.

Singleton, O., B. K. Hölzel, M. Vangel, N. Brach, J. Carmody, and S. W. Lazar. 2014. "Change in Brainstem Gray Matter Concentration Following a Mindfulness-Based Intervention Is Correlated with Improvement in Psychological Well-Being." *Frontiers in Human Neuroscience* 8: Article 33.

# Real change *is* possible

For more than forty-five years, New Harbinger has published proven-effective self-help books and pioneering workbooks to help readers of all ages and backgrounds improve mental health and well-being, and achieve lasting personal growth. In addition, our spirituality books offer profound guidance for deepening awareness and cultivating healing, self-discovery, and fulfillment.

Founded by psychologist Matthew McKay and Patrick Fanning, New Harbinger is proud to be an independent, employee-owned company. Our books reflect our core values of integrity, innovation, commitment, sustainability, compassion, and trust. Written by leaders in the field and recommended by therapists worldwide, New Harbinger books are practical, accessible, and provide real tools for real change.

**Deborah Sosin, MSW, LICSW,** is a writer, editor, and licensed independent clinical social worker specializing in mindfulness and addictions. From 2004 to 2022, she was an outpatient clinician at Sameem Associates in Newton, MA. She also served as a clinical supervisor at the North Charles Institute for the Addictions, and was on the clinical faculties of the MSW programs at Boston College, Simmons College, and Boston University. A graduate of Smith College School for Social Work, Deborah holds an advanced certificate in mindfulness-based psychotherapy from the Institute for Meditation and Psychotherapy. Her picture book, *Charlotte and the Quiet Place,* won several national awards. Her essays have appeared in *The* New York Times, Boston Globe Magazine, Salon, Cognoscenti, and numerous other publications. Deborah lives in the Greater Boston, MA, area.

Foreword writer **Christopher Germer, PhD,** is a clinical psychologist, lecturer on psychiatry at Harvard Medical School, and codeveloper of the Mindful Self-Compassion program with Kristin Neff, which has been taught to more than 250,000 people worldwide. He is coauthor of *The Mindful Path to Self-Compassion,* and maintains a small psychotherapy practice in Cambridge, MA.

# MORE BOOKS from
# NEW HARBINGER PUBLICATIONS

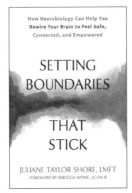

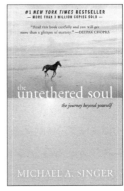

# Did you know there are **free tools** you can download for this book?

Free tools are things like **worksheets, guided meditation exercises**, and **more** that will help you get the most out of your book.

You can download free tools for this book—whether you bought or borrowed it, in any format, from any source—from the New Harbinger website. All you need is a NewHarbinger.com account. Just use the URL provided in this book to view the free tools that are available for it. Then, click on the "download" button for the free tool you want, and follow the prompts that appear to log in to your NewHarbinger.com account and download the material.

You can also save the free tools for this book to your **Free Tools Library** so you can access them again anytime, just by logging in to your account! Just look for this button on the book's free tools page.

**+ Save this to my free tools library**

If you need help accessing or downloading free tools, visit **newharbinger.com/faq** or contact us at **customerservice@newharbinger.com**.